MW00476546

OPRAH'S
JESUS

Prison Book Project
P.O. Box 1146
Sharpes, FL 32959

ANOTHER BOOK BY KURT BRUNER

The Twilight Phenomenon

AVAILABLE FROM DESTINY IMAGE PUBLISHERS

Oprah's Jesus

The Rise of Spirituality Without Religion

Kurt Bruner

Ambient.
An Imprint of
Destiny Image® Publishers, Inc.
P.O. Box 310
Shippensburg, PA 17257

This book and all other Destiny Image, Revival Press, MercyPlace, Fresh Bread, Destiny Image Fiction, and Treasure House books are available at Christian bookstores and distributors worldwide.

For a U.S. bookstore nearest you, call 1-800-722-6774.
For more information on foreign distributors, call 717-532-3040.
Reach us on the Internet: www.destinyimage.com.

ISBN 13 Trade Paper: 978-0-7684-3139-1
ISBN 13 Hardcover: 978-0-7684-3434-7
ISBN 13 Large Print: 978-0-7684-3435-4
ISBN 13 E-book: 978-0-7684-9084-8

For Worldwide Distribution, Printed in the U.S.A.

1 2 3 4 5 6 / 14 13 12 11 10

Contents

INTRODUCTION

SPIRITUAL VERSUS RELIGIOUS

AS A PASTOR, I SUPPOSE I qualify as a fairly "religious" person. I hesitate to say so because, to be honest, the word *religion* carries some pretty negative baggage. Perhaps that's why so many of us describe our "spiritual journey" rather than our "organized religion." The former suggests open-minded enlightenment; the latter, inquisitions and sexual-abuse scandals.

Despite my religious bias, it may ease your mind to know that my official title is "Pastor of Spiritual Formation." That means I help people take the next steps toward exploring and pursuing Christian faith. You won't find "torture heretics" or "cover-up scandals" listed anywhere on my job description. You will, however, find me keenly interested in what people believe—and how those beliefs influence their attitudes and actions.

Oprah's Jesus

When it comes to religion in our generation, one of the most respected voices around is not a pastor, evangelist, priest, or rabbi. She is a warm, articulate woman whose presence dominates television and grocery store check-out stands. Her influence has propelled little-known authors into best-selling millionaires and spawned a media empire worth billions. She is instantly recognized by millions of adoring fans who view her as a long-term friend and trusted spiritual mentor. Her name, of course, is Oprah Winfrey.

Despite what a few angry critics have written in the blogosphere or posted on YouTube—it is unlikely that Oprah's job description lists any troubling items either. She is not, as some have suggested, the leader of a cult. Nor is she head of "the church of Oprah." She is simply a very popular personality who has used her platform to create a kinder, gentler daytime television culture. Jerry Springer reminded us of our worst selves by featuring cheating lovers and catfights dripping with ugly, angry venom. Oprah, by contrast, built an audience using thought-provoking discussion and feel-good moments. She has become the sister, aunt, friend, and self-improvement coach every woman wants.

In addition to bringing us a different kind of talk show, Oprah has begun to champion a different kind of spirituality. She frowns on narrow-minded dogmatism often associated with traditional religion. She instead fans the flame of a more generic spirituality that affirms various paths to enlightenment and questions whether God can fit into a single religious box. In her words, "There couldn't possibly be just one way."[1]

As you might expect, critics pounce on such comments and

make rather harsh accusations—including many who say Oprah has denied Jesus. It is in this context that I was asked to write a book that tries to answer two questions.

> Question 1: *When it comes to religion, what does Oprah believe?* Is her spiritual perspective consistent with a Christian understanding of God, humanity, Jesus, and the rest? And if different, might it be an improvement by freeing us from the harsh fundamentalism associated with organized religion?

> Question 2: *Does it really matter?* Isn't it best to "live-and-let-live" rather than perpetuate cycles of religious intolerance? Does affirming one religious creed over another betray the spirit of love Jesus embodied and taught?

These questions are not new. Nor is Oprah the only celebrity to prompt dialogue about spiritual themes. But she is one of the most influential voices of our time. And she has featured guests and gurus who have invited fans and critics alike to dive a bit deeper into the wonderful mystery of our religious impulse. As a pastor of spiritual formation, I welcome the opportunity to join that dialogue and, I hope, help bridge some of the chasm between the "many paths" and "one way" camps. Toward that end I will serve as your spiritual journey tour guide. We will visit three sites.

In Part I, we will explore the teachings of prominent spiritual leaders who advocate spirituality without religion. I will let them speak for themselves by summarizing their writings and comments in a manner that makes it easy to compare their main ideas to the teachings of Christianity.

In Part II, you will eavesdrop on my conversations with ordinary people who have been influenced by these ideas. We will sit across the table from them and truly listen, hoping to understand why they find Christianity so hard to swallow.

In Part III, I will do my best to explain where "many paths" spirituality aligns with and differs from "one way" Christianity. I'll also explain how "one faith" became so many different denominations.

Whether you are part of a formal religious group or not, I hope you find these pages helpful as you take the next steps on your spiritual journey.

PART I

MANY PATHS

CHAPTER 1

A NEW EARTH

THE PUBLISHING INDUSTRY OFFERS EAGER readers over 300,000 new English book titles each and every year[1]—placing well over seven million titles on our "so many books, so little time" lists.[2] That's why every publisher and author on the planet covets a nod from Oprah's Book Club. When she selects and recommends a book to her audience, it creates a rare publishing sensation, turning otherwise obscure titles into best-sellers high up the Amazon.com sales rankings. Consider just a few of the 67 novels and authors to benefit from this phenomenon:

- *Paradise* by Toni Morrison (1998 Selection)
- *I Know This Much Is True* by Wally Lamb (1998 Selection)
- *A Map of the World* by Jane Hamilton (1999 Selection)

- *The Reader* by Bernhard Schlink (1999 Selection)
- *The Pilot's Wife* by Anita Shreve (1999 Selection)
- *The Poisonwood Bible* by Barbara Kingsolver (2000 Selection)
- *Gap Creek* by Robert Morgan (2000 Selection)
- *The Good Earth* by Pearl S. Buck (2004 Selection)
- *The Road* by Cormac McCarthy (2007 Selection)
- *Middlesex* by Jeffrey Eugenides (2007 Selection)
- *The Story of Edgar Sawtelle* by David Wroblewski (2008 Selection)

Those who consider themselves "readers" probably recognize many of the roughly five dozen titles recommended by the Oprah Book Club. Why, amid millions of potential titles and authors, do so many of us pick from this tiny collection? Two reasons. First, because the most powerful marketing for any book or film is a recommendation from someone we trust and admire. Second, and perhaps even more importantly, because we yearn for community. Oprah's Book Club gives us a chance to transform the solitary experience of reading into something that connects us to others, something that draws us out of our isolated existence into forums that help us relate to others—similar to joining a women's Bible study group at church.

In 2008 Oprah selected the first book in the religious genre—making her club even more like a Bible study group. Rather than the Scriptures, however, she invited readers to discuss the teachings of a spiritual mentor named Eckhart Tolle, author of the book *A New Earth—Awakening to Your Life's Purpose*. Tolle became an overnight sensation after Oprah interviewed him on television and became the catalyst for launching her first-ever online Webcast to discuss spiritual themes outside the constraints of any organized religious institution. She has since launched other popular forums such as the *Oprah.com Spirit Channel* and podcasts featuring "leading spiritual thinkers, teachers and authors" talking about "matters of the soul, spirit and self."[3]

We should respect Oprah's spiritual journey enough to let it speak for itself. Part I of this book is dedicated to listening to some of the spiritual mentors in her life, those she has most enthusiastically recommended to her fans. We begin with Eckhart Tolle.

Introducing her first "worldwide, interactive event" that served as a virtual classroom on all things spiritual, Oprah Winfrey described the Eckhart Tolle forum as "the most exciting thing I've ever done" and as a "global community to talk about what I believe is one of the most important subjects and presented by one of the most important books of our time."

We begin our exploration of Oprah's Jesus by diving into Tolle's book *A New Earth* because she chose it as most representative of her beliefs.[4]

Listening to interviews with and reading the writings of Eckhart and Oprah's other spiritual mentors offers us a remarkably consistent perspective when answering the basic questions every religion must address including:

- Who or what is God?
- Who are we and what is our purpose on this earth?
- What is wrong with our world and how can it be fixed?

- Who is Jesus?
- What does it mean to live a good life?

I should state that Eckhart Tolle and the others featured by Oprah would be reluctant to offer dogmatic answers to any of these questions because they hope to avoid any hint of "one way" religious superiority. But they provide more than enough clarity to discover a common "creed" summarizing what they consider the preferred spiritual path.

Eckhart Tolle's life could be described as a religious "rags to riches" story. Details are a bit cryptic, but I've managed to piece together key scenes. Tolle says he walked away from "a promising academic career" before the age of 30 due to "a profound inner transformation" that radically altered the course of his life. The next few years were spent virtually homeless as he lived off savings while writing his first book. A winning $1,000 lottery ticket bought him just enough time to finish the manuscript before going completely broke.[5]

Eckhart Tolle's official Website states that he spent the next few years "devoted to understanding, integrating and deepening" his transformation which he describes as an "intense inward journey." Later, he worked in London as a counselor and spiritual teacher with individuals and small groups.

One decade and several Oprah interviews later we find Eckhart Tolle doing quite well. He published what he describes as "two of the most influential spiritual books of our time" titled *The Power of Now* and *A New Earth*. These books became the foundation for a growing emphasis in the Oprah media-empire. What are the "big ideas" fueling this emphasis? To quote Tolle's Website:

Eckhart's profound yet simple teachings have already helped countless people throughout the world find inner peace and greater fulfillment in their lives. At the core of the teachings lies the transformation of consciousness, a spiritual awakening that he sees as the next step in human evolution. An essential aspect of this awakening consists in transcending our ego-based state of consciousness. This is a prerequisite not only for personal happiness but also for the ending of violent conflict endemic on our planet.[6]

Those of us raised in a more traditional religious context may find themselves both intrigued and confused by this summary; intrigued because "inner peace and greater fulfillment" sound appealing; confused because we're not accustomed to phrases like "transcending our ego-based state of consciousness." Let's take a look at these and other big ideas developed in Tolle's teachings in order to better understand the "many paths" religious perspective.

THE GOAL: SPIRITUAL AWAKENING

"Spiritual awakening" is a central idea in Eckhart Tolle's teachings. *A New Earth* even carries the subtitle "Awakening to Your Life's Purpose." Some Christians may associate the phrase with an 18th-century movement known as the "Great Awakening" when Christian ministers like Jonathan Edwards and George Whitefield made emotional appeals for sinners to repent and spawned social causes such as the abolition of slavery. But there is no connection. What Tolle means by "awakening" is something entirely different. "This book's main purpose is not to add new information or beliefs to your mind…," he writes, "but to bring about a shift in consciousness, that is to say, to awaken."[7] Awaken to what? To seeing nearly everything in a whole new light. For example:

- Flowers should be seen as "messengers from another realm" serving to bridge the gap between formless ideals and the material world. Along with crystals, precious stones, birds and other "life forms" they become "temporary manifestations of the underlying one Life, one Consciousness."[8]

- We need to move beyond such physical, visible manifestations and outer forms in order to become aware of "the inner essence" present in all living things.[9]

- Traditional religions emphasize outward behavior. But we can't become good by trying to do good things. We rather allow the goodness already within to emerge.[10]

- We can let go of the forms, dogma, and belief systems of traditional religion in order to discover that being "spiritual" has nothing to do with belief or behavior and "everything to do with your state of consciousness."[11]

- The "deeper interconnectedness" of everything tells us that labels such as "good" and "bad" are illusory.[12]

How do we awaken to such a state of spiritual consciousness? Before answering that question, we must discover what put us to sleep in the first place.

THE PROBLEM: EGO

Nobody likes arrogant people. So we nod in agreement when religious leaders condemn stuck-up haughtiness. Both Judaism and Christianity include *pride* among the seven deadly sins. So we will likely resonate with Eckhart Tolle when he describes *ego* as our primary problem. But his definition of *ego* is entirely different from the vice of vanity commonly assumed. He does not condemn thinking too highly of oneself at all. He rather condemns thinking too little of oneself.

Look in the dictionary and you'll find two different concepts behind the English word *ego.* Yes, it can mean "conceit." But the psychological meaning includes "the individual as aware of himself" and more simply "the self." Going further, it includes the part of us which governs our actions rationally.[13]

Awakening to your life's purpose, according to Eckhart Tolle, means freeing yourself from personal identity, physical reality, or a system of rational beliefs. It means solving our chief problem, the illusion of identity. As he explains it:

- We need to "rise above identification with form that keeps the ego in place" and in the process condemns us to "imprisonment" within our individual personalities. Using the words "I" or "me" perpetuates error because doing so embodies "a misperception of who you are, an illusory sense of identity" which is the ego.[14]

- While Christianity teaches that we are all tainted by "original sin" it misses the point. Sin is not to "miss the mark" of belief or behavior, but rather to "to miss the point" of human existence through "identification with forms"—physical, thought and emotional.[15]

- We all experience a measure of "collective insanity" because we are products of a human history that could be diagnosed as "criminally insane, with a few brief lucid intervals." At the root of this insanity has been our identification with "ego."[16]

- Religions are part of our problem because they are by definition belief systems that enslave the ego to rational thought. The founding personalities of each religion may have given humanity a "brief lucid interval" by inviting us into the unity of oneness. But later generations turned those religions into "divisive rather than unifying forces" by becoming belief systems that allowed us to make ourselves "right" and others "wrong."[17]

- Thinking rationally is also part of our problem because it "cuts reality up into lifeless fragments" rather than "sense the interconnectedness of all that exists."[18]

- If evil has any reality, it has a relative, not an absolute, reality. And that *evil* is best defined as the "original sin" of being unaware of our "connectedness with the whole" and our "intrinsic oneness with every 'other' as well as with the Source."[19]

In short, Tolle believes each of us needs to awaken from the illusion of distinct identities, forms, and beliefs so that we can connect to a formless, nonrational consciousness. Our chief problem has been viewing ourselves as individuals when we should view ourselves as part of the "unmanifested one Life" rooted in our "common divinity."[20] We haven't been viewing ourselves too highly. We've forgotten our true grandeur. The solution? Awakening to a spiritual journey labeled "higher consciousness."

THE PATH: HIGHER CONSCIOUSNESS

Unlike spiritual awakenings of the past, says Tolle, the new spirituality is arising largely outside the structures and teachings of institutionalized religions. He says that many former followers of traditional religion have "let go of identification with form, dogma, and rigid belief systems" in order to discover traces of an "original depth" hidden within those traditions and within themselves. These people have come to realize "that how 'spiritual' you are has nothing to do with what you believe but everything to do with your state of consciousness."[21]

For those of us still living in the context of institutionalized religions, phrases such as "state of consciousness" can seem ambiguous. What is it, and how does it provide a path out of the sleepy prison of ego?

- The one most of us call "God" Tolle calls "consciousness."[22] Don't think of God as a separate, distinct creator. He/she/it is more like a giant puzzle. Each of us, along with all other living things, is a small piece contributing to the total picture called "God."

- This new spiritual awakening is not a new belief system, religion, ideology, or mythology. Such things are coming to an end as more people realize that "all religions are equally false and equally true" depending on how you use them. Since we have used them to defend fixed creeds and ego identities, we are better off leaving them behind.[23]

• What about the afterlife? Is there such a place as Heaven or hell? According to Tolle, Heaven is not a distinct location, but "the inner realm of consciousness."[24] We should not depend upon religiously rooted beliefs or behaviors to gain what could be. We should instead rest in the peaceful contentment of what is.

• Eckhart Tolle distrusts anything fixed—including clarifying statements of belief like those found in ancient creeds and sacred texts. He instead celebrates views denounced by traditional religious hierarchies such as Gnosticism, which he says broke free of the "deadening conceptualization and mental belief structures" to emphasize "realization and inner transformation." In Tolle's view, this small minority of mystics "regained the transformative power of the original teachings" in opposition to dominant teachings of Christianity and other organized religions. He says that traveling the path toward "higher consciousness" requires learning to do likewise.[25]

• In addition to abandoning our fixed system of beliefs, higher consciousness means transcending our physical bodies. In other words, we are to rise above the limitations of our embodied existence by releasing any "body-identification" to connect to the "life energy" that allows us to cross the bridge from "form" to "formlessness." This can happen as we see our "essential identity as formless, as an all-pervasive Presence, of Being prior to all forms, all identifications."[26]

- Identification with fixed beliefs and forms imprisons us to the "illusion" of ego. The good news, says Tolle, is that when we recognize the illusion as illusion, it will dissolve. When you realize the impermanence of all forms, you awaken to "the dimension of the formless within yourself, that which is beyond death" which is "eternal life."[27]

- So what, specifically, can we do to gain this kind of higher consciousness? First, "lose yourself" by de-emphasizing your specific form or identity. Second, let the consciousness of your higher, formless identity flow through you by denying time. Tolle calls time "a mental construct" that we can rise above to live in the present moment. "When doing becomes infused with the timeless quality of Being," says Tolle "that is success."[28]

For those of us accustomed to clear statements of belief and the fixed reality of an embodied existence, Eckhart Tolle's teachings can seem confusing. At times it feels like straining to understand a person who speaks in broken English. "Did I hear him wrong, or did he use a foreign word?"

Tolle offers some insight about this difficulty when he writes about one of our primary problems tied to ego: rational thought. "Reality is a unified whole," he explains in the final chapter of *A New Earth*, "but thought cuts it up into fragments. This gives rise to fundamental misperceptions, for example, that there are separate things and events, or that this is the cause of that. Every thought implies a perspective, and every perspective, by its very nature, implies limitation, which ultimately means that it is not true, at least not absolutely. Only the whole is true, but the whole cannot be spoken or thought."[29] This is why he said at the start of the book that he did not seek to "convince you of anything" but rather shift your consciousness through an awakening.[30]

In light of such a claim, critics might ask why Tolle bothers using words to write books and teach his beliefs. Don't his ideas also "cut into fragments" the mystery of the whole? Isn't his perception of reality equally false? To my knowledge, he has never addressed these questions.

Before moving on to other voices in what Oprah calls her "preferred genre of spirituality,"[31] we should pause to summarize Eckhart Tolle's teachings for later reflection. How does the perspective taught in *A New Earth* answer the following common religious questions?

ECKHART TOLLE IN BRIEF

QUESTION: WHO OR WHAT IS GOD?

Tolle's Answer: What we call "God" is an all-en-compassing life-energy that has no distinct form or identity. Each of us is a small part of this overarching, collective consciousness.

QUESTION: WHO ARE WE, AND WHAT IS OUR PURPOSE ON THIS EARTH?

Tolle's Answer: Each of us is a small part of an over-arching, collective consciousness. Our purpose on this earth is to bring a new dimension into this world by living in conscious oneness with the totality and conscious alignment with universal intelligence.

QUESTION: WHO IS JESUS?

Tolle's Answer: Jesus is one of the spiritual "mes-sengers" throughout human history, like Buddha and others, who have tried to bring a message of transformation. His followers, however, largely misunderstood and often greatly distorted His message.

QUESTION: WHAT IS WRONG WITH OUR WORLD AND HOW CAN IT BE FIXED?

Tolle's Answer: The problem is the illusion of "ego" causing us to find identity in rigid beliefs and fixed forms. This is overcome by remembering our essential identity as part of "God," more accurately called "consciousness."

QUESTION: WHAT DOES IT MEAN TO LIVE A GOOD LIFE?

Tolle's Answer: Become part of a new species arising on the planet through an awakened consciousness.[32]

CHAPTER 2

THE SPIRITUAL ADVENTURE

WHEN OPRAH NEEDS A PINCH hitter to host an interview or lead a discussion on the *Oprah and Friends Spirit Network,* she shares her microphone with friend and "fellow spiritual adventurer" Elizabeth Lesser, author of several books including *The Seeker's Guide: Making Your Life a Spiritual Adventure.*

Elizabeth Lesser was the co-founder and a driving force at the Omega Institute, an organization that specializes in the fields of "emotional intelligence" and "healing self and healing society." As a popular author and media personality, she is less active in the day-to-day operations of Omega, but continues as an active board member and advisor to the organization. Lesser's official biography describes her as a *New York Times* best-selling author, speaker, and frequent host on the Oprah & Friends Sirius/XM radio channel. A graduate of San Francisco State University, she is a former midwife and birth educator who taught workshops on emotional intelligence, meditation, women's issues, and death and dying. More recently she has appeared on national radio and television, and lectured at college campuses, retreat centers, and conferences nationwide.[1]

Lesser has a gentle, reflective tone that makes her easier to understand than Eckhart Tolle. Her books carry more substance as she describes the ups and downs of her own spiritual adventure while sharing insights from a variety of mythic and religious traditions.

From the start, Lesser explains that the path of one's spiritual adventure is unique to each individual because it comes from "the hard knocks of daily life and the hard work of self-examination" in addition to "solitary retreats and meetings with remarkable teachers." Elizabeth Lesser's own adventure began in the tumultuous 1960s. "When I was a child God was dead" she explains in reference to the famous 1966 *Time* magazine cover that asked *Is God Dead?* "I was raised in a family and a culture that were hooked on science and progress, and suspicious of spirituality and introspection." In her family, magazines like *National Geographic* and *The New Yorker* replaced Scripture as the source of authority and wisdom at home. Her father worked in the advertising business. He grew up in a nonpracticing Jewish family. Her mother rejected the strict beliefs of devout Christian Science parents. Both of them resented all shades of organized religion, so they raised Elizabeth and her sisters with absolutely no belief system or formal religious training. The clear message: "Intelligent people do not take religion seriously."[2]

But Elizabeth couldn't suppress her fascination with and desire for spirituality. Several encounters fed her interest, such as spending time with her best friend's Italian Catholic family and attending their wonderfully mysterious Mass where people partook of the body and blood of Christ and learning members could share their darkest secrets with a priest during confession. "I wanted to belong to this religion." She recalls.

By the time Lesser turned 14 years old, the *Time* magazine article and her lack of spiritual belonging created an odd sense of loss because God had died "before making formal contact with me."

Over time she came to understand that what she sensed, the loss she felt from an early age, reflected a shifting pendulum in Western spirituality, from submission to a "judging, parental god" to the "autonomous individual" who turned personal progress and materialism into the religion of the West. The pendulum went too far, creating a sense of isolation in Elizabeth and a "yearning for a spiritual life and the sense of belonging to something greater than my personal world."

So, as a young adult, she defied her parents' secular perspective—but retained their disaffiliation with traditional western faiths. So her first steps toward spirituality were gleaned from Zen Buddhism and other Eastern religious traditions.[3] Elizabeth and her future husband found themselves drawn to a range of Eastern religious practices including Hindi yoga and incense laden meditation which gave her a "strange sense of peaceful dignity." Hanging out in their favorite esoteric bookstore in Greenwich Village, they encountered writings from a variety of nontraditional spiritual movements—each seeking direct access to the divine and carrying traces of past influences from Buddhist monks in India, Gnosticism, Neoplatonism, and Islam.[4]

In 1972, at the age of 19, Elizabeth went from New York to California to live in a communal "Sufi camp." She describes that summer as a time when she "embraced the spiritual path of Sufism" that included initiation through study, meditation, prayer, and right behavior. As one who had never experienced the commitment and support of a Christian or Jewish congregation, "this kind of spiritual flock seemed an exotic variation on my childhood dreams."[5]

She had found a form of spirituality that seemed open to the entire spectrum of humanity's religious impulse. A given Sunday service might include readings from the Koran, Hindu, and Buddhist texts, Sufi stories, even selections from the Old and New Testaments of the Bible. Afterward they might chant mantras or perform a traditional Jewish dance before following the example of Jesus by washing one another's feet. And they would always "meditate, focusing on the breath and silently repeating the ninety-nine beautiful names of Allah" which is a traditional Islamic practice.[6]

"This immersion in religious tradition was thrilling to me." Lesser said of this period. "My childhood curiosity and hunger were being addressed in ways I had never ever imagined. What I had intuited—that it is human nature to hunger for the sacred—was being revealed in a rich tapestry of myth and traditions from around the world. God may have died in mainstream culture, but spirituality was being revived in my life through the traditional and proven practices of world religions."[7]

A few years after marrying her boyfriend and starting a family, Elizabeth Lesser left the rigors of the commune, but that season imprinted her with a spiritual perspective that continues to shape her teachings more than three decades later. In 1977 she helped launch the Omega Institute, a place one observer described as "where all thought converged" as humans evolve "toward a more enlightened consciousness."[8]

Another season of Lesser's spiritual journey was marked by pain. She admits to sexual promiscuity before marriage, leading to an abortion, an extramarital affair that contributed to her divorce, the challenges and stigma of single motherhood, and the lingering regret of shaming her parents. These experiences led her to seek a therapist who could help her combine "psychological growth, emotional wisdom, and physical and sexual healing." This part of the journey generated interest in Jungian psychology and the corresponding study of world mythology.[9]

Lesser's recent work merges her religious adventure and healing journey by focusing on holistic health, psychology, and cross-cultural arts and religion. The end result is something she describes as a uniquely American form of spirituality.

THE NEW AMERICAN SPIRITUALITY

Elizabeth Lesser believes we have witnessed the birth of a new form of spirituality, one distinctly American. This form of spirituality, like the melting pot persona of the nation, is characterized by a fierce independence that elevates individuality and autonomy over almost any other virtue. We see it in the explosive growth of non-denominational and nonaffiliated

Christian, Jewish, Buddhist, and Islamic congregations. We see it in a near universal reticence to submit to any religious hierarchy or denominational oversight. This emerging spirituality, as Lesser explains, "crosses religious and social boundaries, telling the tale of a diverse people, gathered in close proximity, and absorbing each other's ways of worshiping, ritualizing, and mythologizing the great mysteries of life. It contains the nature-centered traditions of the original peoples of the Americas. It is part science…respects both a mistrust of heavy-handed authority and the willing surrender to a greater power…draws from the religious teachings of the past…" as well as "the wisdom of psychology, democracy and feminism."[10]

What does this new spirituality offer? To find out we will use the same three categories that helped us understand Eckhart Tolle's teachings.

THE GOAL: YOUR OWN ADVENTURE

Lesser wholeheartedly endorses the "many paths" philosophy of religious inquiry. "A good thing to remember as we search for our own definition of spirituality" she explains, "is that no one has *the* definition of *the* answers to the most basic spiritual questions of how to live, love and die."[11]

You might find such a statement disheartening. After all, what is the point of asking questions if you know answers can't be found? But Lesser considers the ambiguity an empowering part of the quest because "the unique and most positive aspect of the new American spirituality is its emphasis on self-authority." She celebrates the shift from any "central, hierarchal authority figure" to what she calls "a democracy of individual seekers" and "the democratizing of spirituality." Rather than an authority describing the path to sacred truth, each individual maps his or her own journey.[12] Rather than purchase a pre-printed city map or click on your GPS to find a specific location, you grab paper and pencil to create a new, unique set of directions.

Lesser seems to go beyond the idea that many roads lead to God. She does more than affirm each person's choice between existing religious traditions such as Christianity, Islam, Judaism, Buddhism, Hinduism, and others. She encourages each individual to construct his or her own religious framework—taking and leaving bits from all or none of the traditional paths. "You can walk a wonderful spiritual path with or without adhering to a religion. All paths are available; none are exclusively right or wrong or even required." And if your religious upbringing limits your ability to define your own form of spirituality, then you should "set aside your religious beliefs and/or resistances."[13] You can always come back to them later if you so choose.

You might say Elizabeth Lesser sees spirituality more like a grocery store than a restaurant. Rather than selecting from a menu of gourmet meals found in existing religious traditions, you get to pick and choose the raw ingredients that fit your own recipe. That way you get to be your own chef or "authority." In her words, "Religions are like cookbooks and guidebooks: they are not the food or the foreign country; rather, they suggest ingredients and point us in the right direction."

She never clarifies what to do if you can't cook or if you prefer the quickest route because she claims to value autonomy over accuracy and adventure over arrival.

The Problem: Seeking Answers

If we hope to become spiritual adventurers, Lesser suggests, we must overcome our tendency to seek answers. We must instead learn to "live the questions."

She explains that we have spent three thousand years looking for answers. And what has this pursuit gotten us? It created the modern schism between religious fundamentalists who "seek comfort in rigid doctrines of their own creation" and scientific fundamentalists who demand proof using "their own intellectual constructs to prove or disprove their own questions."[14]

The common error of both groups, suggests Lesser, is that they expect to find answers. In other words, we approach God and spirituality using our minds rather than "a different sort of consciousness."[15] Like people living in the valley between two mountain ranges, we hear the echoes beyond—but can't make out what is being said. We use our favorite listening device, the logical mind. But the logical mind is inadequate for the task. "Like great scientific problems," Lesser suggests "great theological ones ask us to step into a consciousness beyond the one we normally inhabit."[16]

Religious dogma contributes to the problem because it tries to answer rather than live the questions. Each religion has become watered down from the original intent of its founder—so it no longer satisfies the spiritual hunger of many. The roots of every religion "are in the soil of sacred experience," but have been co-opted by "power-hungry people" who exploit religion to gain a sense of control over others."[17] In Lesser's view, Jesus and other religious founders did not intend to answer our questions in ways that would empower an institution. They instead serve as models for those who would empower themselves.

Elizabeth considers the 17th century a turning point in how humanity approached ultimate questions. Philosophers such as Rene Descartes gave us new lenses through which to view ourselves. Rather than seeing human behavior as the choice between faith in God and submission to the devil, the modern era enabled us to conceive of human reason and choices "outside the realm of the Church." This perspective eventually led to more "scientific" disciplines such as psychology, in which Lesser finds useful tools for humanizing spirituality.

But the enlightenment also enabled the other side of the schism—a strictly scientific perspective that discounts all spiritual realities or considerations. Rather than seek answers through submission to religious authority, it seeks answers using human reason. It simply moved the problem—taking authority away from religious institutions and handing it to the intellectual elite. It is another version of the same disempowering problem.

THE PATH: SEEKING NEW CONSCIOUSNESS

How does one break free of the desire for answers and move down the seeker's path? Elizabeth Lesser recommends taking all religious practices seriously without submitting to the dogmatic beliefs of any of them. A new state of consciousness is achieved by "tranquil abiding" rather than active inquiry, by connecting with one's "spiritual longing" rather than reaching a clear destination.

"Spirituality is the human search for eternal wisdom." Lesser explains. "It is not the wisdom itself." Remember, we are not seeking answers—we are living the questions. And that process looks different for every person. Some of us will respond better to one religious ritual or meditation technique than others. The key is for each person to find his or her own unique path.

To her credit, Lesser criticizes many glib seekers for trivializing "powerful and elegant" spiritual growth systems when they "skim off the ritual trappings of a tradition with little respect for the depth behind it." She tries to distance herself from such practices and people who behave like "drunk honeybees" flitting from one religious flower to the next rather than "carefully creating a path that includes genuine practices from a variety of traditions."[18]

Despite encouraging each person to map his or her own journey, Elizabeth Lesser recommends a path toward a spirituality of wholeness by describing four specific arenas or "landscapes" within which seekers can grow.

THE LANDSCAPE OF MIND

Like Eckhart Tolle, Elizabeth Lesser finds "ego" a major obstacle to spiritual growth. Again, this is not simple arrogance but any sense of individual, personal identity apart from the greater oneness of which all living beings are part. "The ego's delusion," she explains "is that each one of us is a separate and finite entity that must fight for self-preservation." She calls the ego a form of gravity that keeps us trapped in the "overidentification with our individuality" and prevents us from embracing "a spirituality that respects both our humanness and our divinity."

How does the mind limit our growth? Again, by trying to

find answers. "What we think we know limits our full potential" says Lesser. That's why we must look deeply "into the nature of things through meditation" enabling us to "see how the false ego makes false assumptions about reality." The simple routine of meditation can help us rise above our individuality because "just knowing that reality is different from what our false ego assumes is liberating."[19]

THE LANDSCAPE OF HEART

Throughout human history we have told stories that include heroes, gods, mythic creatures, and magical beings. According to Jungian philosophy—all great stories follow a similar pattern because they bubble up from a common human narrative. We love to tell and hear stories because they help us connect our individual journeys to the universal experiences of grief, joy, loss, and love. Something similar happens through music, poetry, art, and other creative expressions. In Lesser's view, these experiences provide a powerful alternative to reason for achieving greater consciousness—"bypassing the cut-and-dried and going straight to the imaginal realms" through "creative visualization" or "guided imagery."[20]

THE LANDSCAPE OF BODY

Unlike many in her genre of spirituality, Elizabeth Lesser seems at ease with the body. Her higher consciousness peers tend to view our physical reality as an illusion to escape rather than as part of our essential being. Lesser's maternal grandparents, for example, embraced a form of spirituality that encouraged people to bypass the body and to treat disease as nothing more than "a bad dream." By contrast, she says that our bodies need appropriate care—and that the body "remembers" the harmful things we do to ourselves—such as her own promiscuity and subsequent abortion. So we need to attend to the body as an important landscape for spiritual healing. "To take thoughtful care of your body is to hone the self-healing abilities you already have."[21]

THE LANDSCAPE OF SOUL

The first three landscapes prepare seekers for the final and most impactful arena for connecting to "the life force" and hearing "the song of the soul." This landscape is the place one's soul connects with the mystery of God. And entering this phase requires "a leap of faith."

I should note that Elizabeth Lesser does not mean "faith" the way most of us understand the word. She says that "faith" and "karma" carry the same meaning. Most of us use "faith" in the context of a personal God who has revealed Himself to us. The concept of karma, by contrast, assumes a pantheistic world governed by an impersonal force.

Understanding this difference in terms, what does Lesser mean by "leap into the landscape of the soul?" She suggests we find clues to the nature of God and the soul everywhere—asking us not "to limit your source of wisdom to one tradition," but to let "what resonates with your own experience spur you on to discover the vast and unified and fundamental consciousness called God."

In other words, the landscape of the soul is the process of adopting "a variety of practices, prayers and rituals to nurture the kind of consciousness that welcomes a vision of God."[22]

How would Elizabeth Lesser answer the five questions every spiritual perspective tries to address? It turns out that her answers are essentially the same as those of Eckhart Tolle's.

ELIZABETH LESSER IN BRIEF

QUESTION: WHO OR WHAT IS GOD?

Lesser's Answer: God is "not one thing or another," but rather flowing "beneath and through all things."[23]

QUESTION: WHO ARE WE, AND WHAT IS OUR PURPOSE ON THIS EARTH?

Lesser's Answer: Each of us is part of the universal "I am" that transcends individual identity.

QUESTION: WHO IS JESUS?

Lesser's Answer: Jesus is one of many religious teachers, like Buddha and Mohammad, who tried to point us to the essential unity of all things. This is what He meant by the unified Trinity of the Father, the Son, and the Holy Spirit—attempting to lead seekers into an experience of unity.[24] His "I am" statements were a way of inviting us to realize we are all one.[25]

QUESTION: WHAT IS WRONG WITH OUR WORLD AND HOW CAN IT BE FIXED?

Lesser's Answer: Our problem is that we are trapped in the illusion of individual identity ("ego"), keeping us from spiritual wholeness. We can heal by creating our own unique spiritual path gleaned from a variety of religious and non-religious practices.

QUESTION: WHAT DOES IT MEAN TO LIVE A GOOD LIFE?

Lesser's Answer: A good life is one of spiritual adventure—gaining wholeness by pursuing your own spiritual path enriched by a variety of religious traditions.

CHAPTER 3

SPIRITUAL LIBERATION

WHILE ECKHART TOLLE and Elizabeth Lesser have been the most prominent spiritual teachers featured by Oprah in recent years, many others have been given a platform to share similar perspectives. Each possesses a unique history, personality, and style. But all advocate a "many paths" perspective on spirituality.

Michael Bernard Beckwith is a handsome, middle-aged man with long dreadlocks who exudes vitality, confidence, and health. I found him appealing from my first glance at his picture on the cover of his recent book. I had never heard of him before doing my research for this book, but he has been a regular on Oprah's Spirit Channel and an articulate teacher who challenges readers to fulfill their soul's potential through what his book title calls *Spiritual Liberation*.

Beckwith speaks to 9,000 regular attendees at the Agape International Spiritual Center, which he founded. He also co-founded the Association for Global New Thought. Through his teaching, writing, and media presence, Beckwith seeks to inspire people toward a spiritual libration that he describes as "discovering and expressing the intrinsic qualities of enlightened consciousness that have been ours since the moment we came into existence."[1]

Like his peers, Beckwith seems reluctant to imply his own views contain the final word on spirituality. He says that his teachings are "not the result of my having reached ultimate spiritual conclusions that I now present as being '*the* truth.' It is rather a summation of my own journey of some thirty years of entering the Great Mystery and exploring frontiers of consciousness...the result of my having discarded a materialistic worldview and replaced it with the realization that a committed spiritual practice illuminates and clarifies our purpose on the planet."[2]

On what path did Beckwith journey toward this great mystery? He says it began in a family dedicated to social activism such as anti-Vietnam protests and efforts to restore social justice in a world of racial inequity.

During the 1970s, he became a psychobiology major at the University of Southern California where he began experimenting with and later selling marijuana. His initial experiences with spirituality came while smoking weed, even though he called himself an agnostic. One day he awoke from a troubling dream in which he had been killed and immediately felt "a magnificent presence" he identified as "Love-Beauty." This experience drove him to abandon dealing drugs and begin studying Eastern and Western mystics to learn more about the "Universal One" he had encountered.[3]

Immediately after this experience, Beckwith had a close call that almost put him in jail for dealing drugs. He got off on a technicality, after which he promised himself "from this moment forward my life is dedicated to serving Love-Beauty in the world."[4] So that's what he has done, eventually becoming a popular spiritual teacher.

Michael Bernard Beckwith strongly advocates a "many paths" religious perspective, claiming that the essential claims of various faiths "are not at odds" because "the closer you get to the heart of their messages there is less contradiction" so that "dogma disappears and religious titles and creeds dissolve."[5]

While Beckwith does not look to the Bible for authority, he does borrow biblical language. In a key affirmation, for example, he credits the spirit of "Love-Beauty" with helping him experience "the peace that surpasseth all understanding." This is a phrase that comes from the old-English, as written in the King James Version of the Bible. In another place he borrows the biblical word *atonement,* saying it means "at-one-ment" with pure Spirit.[6] Use of such terminology might cause some to assume he affirms orthodox Christian beliefs. But he would make no such claim. What, specifically, does he teach?

THE GOAL: SPIRITUAL ENLIGHTENMENT

We find our life purpose and realize our soul's potential when we "co-create our lives in harmony with the laws govern-

45

ing the universe. This natural expression of our innate wholeness is enlightenment."[7] Beckwith believes the "intrinsic qualities of enlightened consciousness" belong to and can be found by each and every person.[8]

THE PROBLEM: EGO-DRIVEN INTELLECT

If enlightened consciousness is a natural part of our existence, what prevents us from experiencing spiritual liberation? According to Beckwith, we let our minds get in the way, chaining us to "identification with the egoic self." In his words, "the roots of our intellect do not reach deeply enough into our spiritual morrow to contact the source and purpose of our existence."[9]

THE PATH: CONSCIOUS ACTIVATION

How do we break free of the limitations of the intellect? "Simply put, all that is required to live up to our highest potential is already inside us awaiting our conscious activation." This awakening is achieved through meditative practices that help us tune our lives to "the evolutionary impulse" that is infinite, conscious, and seeks to articulate itself by means of us."[10] Put another way, achieving our potential "is about becoming more ourselves, more of who and what we are as awakened beings."[11]

While his terminology may be slightly different, Beckwith's core ideas bear a remarkable similarity to the teachings of Tolle and Lesser. His answers to the five key questions affirm the same essential worldview.

MICHAEL BERNARD BECKWITH IN BRIEF

QUESTION: WHO OR WHAT IS GOD?

Beckwith's Answer: A mysterious presence that permeates all things and that is everywhere in its fullness.[12]

QUESTION: WHO ARE WE, AND WHAT IS OUR PURPOSE ON THIS EARTH?

Beckwith's Answer: Our "Authentic Self" is our "original face" as inherently enlightened beings which Christians define as "soul."[13]

QUESTION: WHO IS JESUS?

Beckwith's Answer: Beckwith calls Jesus "the Christ," but does not use the word to mean "messiah" or "savior" as might be assumed. He rather sees Jesus as one of many mystics who gave us a taste of "the Infinite" and opened our awareness to "a dynamic Presence that is the life force enlivening all that there is."[14]

QUESTION: WHAT IS WRONG WITH OUR WORLD AND HOW CAN IT BE FIXED?

Beckwith's Answer: We have stalled on our way toward full enlightenment and need to consciously participate in our evolution.[15]

QUESTION: WHAT DOES IT MEAN TO LIVE A GOOD LIFE?

Beckwith's Answer: We live a good life when we trust the "revelations and insights" that knock at the door of our awareness and let them lead us toward "further openings of consciousness."[16]

CHAPTER 4

NON-RELIGIOUS?

ECKHART TOLLE, ELIZABETH LESSER, AND Michael Bernard Beckwith each possess a distinct personality offering spiritual guidance with a unique style and emphasis. But as we've discovered, they overlap a great deal when it comes to the foundational questions every worldview must address. I highlight these three out of many spiritual teachers Oprah has featured because they are fairly representative of her "preferred genre of spirituality." This "genre" carries a variety of labels including New Age and Eastern Mysticism. Once you know what to look for, you will discern the same basic themes in the teachings of many, many others.

Reverend Ed Bacon, for example, serves as the Rector of All Saints Episcopal Church in Pasadena, California. Featured prominently by Oprah, Bacon's inclusion seems to suggest traditional Christian denominations share the basic assumptions of the "many paths" spiritual perspective. For example, while serving on a panel discussion alongside Elizabeth Lesser and Michael Bernard Beckwith, Reverend Bacon said it is an illusion to believe we are distinct, separate individuals from God, separate from one another, or separate from anything else that exists. "Spirituality is about wholeness of our being connected with ourselves, with everyone else, with all that is and with God."

When asked to explain further, Bacon did not quote traditional Christian teachings at all. He rather summarized ideas expressed by Elizabeth Lesser and others by explaining that, "When we are connected with the divine intelligence, which is all there is, we become intelligent and we become connected with all there is. We experience the all-ness, the oneness, the wholeness that God is and that we are."[1]

Reverend Bacon's ideas are not unique among liberal Christian clergy. In fact, they owe much to the writings of fellow Episcopal minister Bishop John Shelby Spong. Bishop Spong has written many books describing his own journey from traditional Christian teachings to a more inclusive spirituality, including the 2007 best-seller *Jesus for the Non-Religious*. After describing his own departure away from traditional forms of Christian worship and belief, Spong lays the groundwork for a Jesus *without* supernatural stories such as feeding the 5,000 or rising from the dead. He also claims to have abandoned the belief in a personal, distinct God commonly labeled *theism*.

In his words, "I hope to find a way through the human Jesus, but beyond the confines of religion, that will lead me into all that I now believe the word 'God' means."[2]

Who is this Jesus for the non-religious and what "God" does he express? Spong answers these questions in a way that opens the door for others to claim a "Christianity" that clearly abandons traditional Christian views.

"What is it that drives me to pry loose from Jesus of Nazareth the layers of supernatural miracles, creedal formulations and ancient mythology?" Spong asks in the opening chapter of his book. "The answer is quite simple: I am a Christian."

He quickly clarifies his definition of Christian. "Many of the things historically said about Jesus I, as one who yearns to be a believer, can no longer hold with credibility." Spong goes on to explain that traditional assertions about Christ's deity "have become for me not only literal nonsense but also little more than theological gobbledygook."[3]

The aging Spong led the way among members of the clergy who overtly side with those rejecting essential Christian beliefs such as the incarnation of Jesus Christ and the resurrection. What does he offer instead? A Jesus very similar to the one upheld by the "many paths" teachers routinely featured by Oprah. I'll let Spong speak for himself:

- "My commitment…is to the reality of Jesus as a God experience."[4]

- "Propositional statements can never capture eternal truth."[5]

- "When I say that God was in Christ or when I assert that I meet God in the person of Jesus, I mean something quite different from the theological definitions of the past that forged doctrines like the incarnation and the trinity, both of which depend upon a theistic definition of God. So in order to get to the essence of who Jesus was and even who Jesus is, I must get beyond the traditional theistic definition of God that I now regard as both simplistic and naive, to say nothing of being wrong."[6]

- "God for me is a reality that can be experienced, but when I try to speak of this experience, I discover that God always transcends the grasp of my explanations. That fact alone drives me beyond any religious system that claims to possess the truth of God in any ultimate sense."[7]

To his credit, Bishop Spong does not pretend to accept orthodox Christian beliefs, making it clear that his definition of God and Jesus come from a different dictionary:

- "God did not come down from some heavenly sphere above the sky to enter human life. Human life emerged into wholeness that was seen as a manifestation of God and was then called divinity. That is what the Jesus experience was all about."[8]

- Jesus is "divine" because "his humanity and his consciousness were so whole and so complete that the meaning of God could flow through him. He was thus able to open people to that transcendent dimension of life, love and being that we call God."[9]

- "Full humanity flows into the divine reality. Divinity becomes and is the ultimate depth of humanity…The meaning and the reality of God are found in the experience of human wholeness flowing in life-giving ways through all that we are. God is experienced when life is opened to transcendent otherness, when it is called beyond every barrier into an ever-expanding human-ity…I anticipate and await Jesus' new explosion into the human consciousness."[10]

Both Bishop Spong and Reverend Bacon remind us that wearing a clerical collar and earning a salary from traditional Christian churches does not necessarily mean you accept Christian teachings about God and Jesus. Those who claim there are many paths to God wear a variety of labels, even if they share the same ideas.

Non-Religious?

An oft repeated theme among those in Oprah's genre of spirituality is the rejection of formal religion, especially traditional Christianity. They believe they have matured beyond seeing God as a bearded, judgmental being ruling the universe from afar. They prefer a more inclusive, non-demanding "God" of which we are all part.

But does this view support the notion they have moved beyond traditional religion? Not really. It simply means they have left one religion for another. You see, each of these spiritual teachers merges ideas found in two very old, very religious traditions—Buddhism and ancient paganism.

Buddhism in Brief

Some may be surprised to learn that modern spiritual

teachers derive their ideas from such an old, traditional faith as Buddhism. If that were the case, wouldn't they look more like the Dalai Lama, complete with shaved heads and Tibetan attire?

Not all Buddhists dress like monks any more than all Christians dress like priests or nuns. In the same way, not everyone who embraces Buddhist philosophy belongs to a Buddhist sect. But a brief summary of Buddhist teachings quickly reveals the source of many concepts taught by Tolle, Lesser, Beckwith, and others. The basic ideas can be found in what Buddhism labels the "Four Noble Truths" which state:

1. *Something is wrong:* Buddhism starts with the recognition that all existence, including human existence, is imperfect in a very deep way.

2. *We know why:* Buddhism teaches that our suffering has an identifiable cause. We all have a fundamental dissatisfaction with what is and reach for something else.

3. *We can free ourselves:* The Buddhist concept of "nirvana" says we can break free of the ego-driven yearnings that keep us enslaved to suffering and individual identities.

4. *There is a path:* Each of us can create fertile soil for reaching nirvana through practical steps such as meditation to achieve greater enlightenment and unlock "the door of the cell of individuality."[11]

Within these "Noble Truths" fit a range of practices and philosophies commonly expressed by modern "many paths" spiritual teachers. For example, Buddhism says every individual must discover his or her own path to enlightenment rather than accept the dogma of any creed. The Buddha himself told a group of his disciples "do not be satisfied with hearsay or with tradition or with legendary lore or with what has come down in your scriptures or with conjecture or with logical inference or with weighing evidence…" He considered such approaches to spirituality "unprofitable" and encouraged each individual to trust his or her own experience over any source of authority.[12]

This perspective dominates the various direct and indirect descendents of traditional Buddhism. "If one reserves the right to find the truth for oneself," writes Buddhist expert John Snelling "one must logically accord the same right to others—and also respect them if they arrive at different conclusions."[13]

Buddhism does not consider specific religious beliefs as competing descriptions of God and reality. It rather treats them as useful launching pads for individual spiritual quests helping us break free from the delusion of individual identity. They hesitate to name or describe this spiritual quest in specific terms because, as Snelling explains, it is "something that cannot be grasped by the intellect or described in words." It can only be experienced directly so that "veils of delusion fall away and at last the world is perceived as it really is. At the same time a deep compassion also crystallizes: a pure, selfless kindliness and caring born of an understanding of the unity of all things."[14]

Even a quick overview of Buddhist concepts helps us connect the dots to modern "many paths" spiritual teachers. They may believe they are celebrating all religions. But in reality, they closely align with the teachings of Buddhism.

PAGANISM

Perhaps the best way to understand why modern spirituality echoes ancient paganism is to revisit a first century conversation. The apostle Paul was interviewed on the Oprah show of his day during a visit to Athens, Greece—the intellectual capital of the world and ancient home to such philosophical giants as Plato and Aristotle (see Acts 17:16-34). Athens also served as the world's religious capital, birthplace to a religious convergence that had come to dominate the Roman Empire.

While on layover to Corinth, Paul entered into dialogue with the city's academic elite—those who no doubt prided themselves on cutting-edge thinking and open-minded acceptance. While he stood on Mars Hill, surrounded by altars celebrating gods from every perspective under the Roman sun, evidence of their religious tolerance literally stared Paul in the face as he presented his own brand of belief. Much like Socrates had done centuries earlier, Paul entered one first-century Starbucks after another to engage in philosophical discourse. Before long, word spread that some Jewish guy from a remote corner of the empire was pushing a new, foreign religion.

"Come and tell us more about this new religion," they said. "You are saying some rather startling things, and we want to know what it's all about."

Keep in mind, discussing the latest ideas is what people in Athens did. Missing the opening of a new philosophy would be as unthinkable as New York critics missing the latest Broadway play. So a crowd quickly gathered to hear Paul make his case.

"Men of Athens, I notice that you are very religious…" Paul must have winked as the audience chuckled at such an understatement, "…for as I was walking along I saw your many altars."

These "many altars" visibly expressed the common view that every religious myth was equally valid because none were necessarily true. Few in the pagan world actually believed their idol to be a deity, especially among the educated class. They saw them as symbols, icons of a greater reality. No one knew which (if any) mythology most accurately reflected the real story of God. So they brought all religious stories together in one place, hoping their collective script might tell the larger story. But instead of connecting the people to the authentically supernatural, they created an extremely superstitious culture.

Paul continues. "And one of these altars had this inscription on it—'To an Unknown God.' You have been worshiping Him without knowing who He is, and now I wish to tell you about Him."

At this point you might have heard a collective gasp of surprise and intrigue. Surprise because few dared claim certain knowledge of the true God, yet intrigue because of Paul's piercing insight into their deeper motives.

Like their hero, Socrates, the Athenians sensed there had to be a real God out there somewhere, even if His particular name and description remained a mystery. When Paul claimed knowledge of this God, ears perked up.

"He is the God who made the world and everything in it. Since He is Lord of heaven and earth, He doesn't live in man-made temples…He himself gives life and breath to everything, and He satisfies every need there is."

After describing the God of all power, Paul made an amazing statement.

"His purpose in all of this was that the nations should seek after God and *perhaps feel their way toward Him and find Him— though He is not far from any of us.*"

Paul knew that deep within every man and woman throbs both the desire and capacity to "feel their way toward" the God who, in Paul's words, "is not far from any of us." Yes, there exists a real God our idols only suggest. He wants to be known. He can be known. Everything we are grows out of the fact that we are His offspring. Paul explains further that God can overlook people's former ignorance, inviting them out of mythic shadows into the light of a true story.

Paul concludes by explaining Jesus' part in that story. Some accepted his message. Others did not. Most wanted to hear more. But all must have walked away from that assembly with eight tiny words ringing in their ears, *"He is not far from any of us."*

Those who appear on television and podcasts or write books celebrating "many paths to God" embrace a notion very similar to the beliefs of those Paul encountered in Athens. Every religion, they believe, is a mythology that points us toward greater spiritual realities. Every spiritual quest, they believe, suggests a common yearning for transcendent reality no matter what form it takes. Even orthodox Christians can join the apostle Paul in affirming these basic ideas. But Paul told the ancient world the good news that the unknown God they worshiped in ignorance had made Himself known in the incarnation of Jesus Christ.

Some would describe Oprah and her spiritual mentors as horribly out of date. They missed the 2,000-year-old memo about the "unknown God" making Himself known to us.

In summary, Oprah's brand of spirituality reflects dominant themes from traditional Buddhism mixed with the "many paths to God" perspective found in ancient paganism. But as we will discover in Part III, it is possible to move beyond uncertainty and superstition. The God of mystery has introduced Himself by the name Jesus Christ. What's more, He made the outrageous claim to be the one and only way.

PART II

SINCERE UNBELIEF

CHAPTER 5

HARD TO SWALLOW

A S I MENTIONED EARLIER, I'M "all in" when it comes to Christian faith. I accept Jesus' claim to be *"the way, the truth, and the life"* (John 14:5-7). But I have spent many hours in sometimes uncomfortable dialogue with friends, relatives, and near strangers who find that claim very hard to swallow. It is relatively easy to sit in the comfort of my reading chair comparing and contrasting the beliefs of modern spiritual gurus with historic Christianity. Things get a bit more difficult when sharing a Starbucks with a sincere, kind-hearted person who doesn't buy the religion I love.

So, in the spirit of Oprah, I thought it would be a good idea to interview several people who left traditional Christianity for a more "inclusive" spirituality. Following Jesus' second command to "love your neighbor as yourself" includes honestly listening to their stories and better understanding their struggles (see Matt. 22:39).

I invite you to sit quietly on the other side of a one-way mirror, observing my dialogue with those who nod in agreement with Oprah's brand of spirituality. What you see and hear may bother you. But there may be moments when you can relate to the misgivings expressed, even hearing your own thoughts in the words of others. Other times you might feel an overwhelming urge to shout through the glass to correct mistaken impressions, refute faulty arguments, or justify actions of the God you adore (I felt the same temptation). But remember, our goal is not to argue, but to listen.

I begin with Mary Ellen.[1]

Mary Ellen sat quietly with the other children on the uncomfortable, rickety wooden folding chairs relegated to the kids. Neither of the congregations in her tiny Appalachian mountain town could afford nice furniture. Grandma attended the "holy roller" church, with lots of shouting, hellfire and brimstone preaching, and speaking in strange, heavenly languages—common in these parts during the early 1950s. But Mary Ellen became frightened attending Sunday school with Grandma, so her parents let her attend the Methodist church, a bit more serious and dignified in its religious expression. Daddy didn't much care. In his opinion, religion would be better off if there were no denominations to cause so much division.

In one of those serious moments in children's church when everyone is asked to bow their heads and close their eyes for prayer and reflection, the minister paused his conversation with God in order to speak directly to the youngsters in a low, somber tone—almost as if the good Lord Himself had prompted a time of inward spiritual examination.

"Children, being open and honest before our heavenly Father, I would like to see the hands of everyone who sinned this past week," the minister began. "The Bible tells us if we confess our sins, God is faithful and just to forgive us our sins. But we must begin with the recognition of our need. So let me see your hands if you know you did something wrong since last Sunday."

During the few moments allotted for reflection, Mary Ellen dutifully rehearsed the past seven days in her mind. At ten-and-a-half years old, opportunities for serious mischief come few and far between. She thought of that moment in gym class when the teacher introduced a form of gymnastics that looked and felt a whole lot like dancing, a Methodist no-no. But Mary Ellen did more awkward stumbling than graceful floating, so that wouldn't make the cut.

On a few occasions she resented being asked to do her chores, but she had checked her attitude so quickly that she doubted whether Mom or Dad took notice. So she scratched those episodes off her mental checklist. She had played no cards, uttered no bad words, thrown no temper tantrums. Mary Ellen had pretty much remained on the straight and narrow all week long. So she kept her hands folded in her lap.

Meanwhile, every other kid had lifted his or her hand (whether from a sense of profound conviction or a desire to satisfy the minister's expectations, remained unclear). Either way, it left Mary Ellen in the unenviable position of being the only self-righteous child in class.

"Mary Ellen!" came the stern, disapproving voice of the minister. "Raise your hand!"

She never forgot that moment. Five decades later she still describes it as embarrassing and confusing. Innocent of the crime, she was ordered to confess her guilt.

The incident symbolizes the disillusionment Mary Ellen has encountered time after time in her attempts to fit into Christianity. She has tried to understand and embrace a faith in which she has never felt entirely at home.

"I would describe myself as a good person," she says. "I had to find a place in the world for myself that is not that strict and not that judgmental."

Now about 60 years old, Mary Ellen radiates a beauty and warmth that well suits her work with geriatric and brain-injured patients. Surprisingly articulate, considering that she grew up in a Smokey Mountain town of 500, Mary Ellen overcame more obstacles and baggage than most to achieve an impressive academic and professional standing.

Mary Ellen works as a counselor. She exudes kindness and compassion, the kind of person anyone would gladly call "friend" or "confidant." Clearly a good listener, she feels a bit awkward being interviewed; she feels more accustomed to hearing from others than taking center stage. But Mary Ellen agreed to help me with the research for my book as one more way she could help others, allowing them to learn from the ups and downs of her own journey, a journey that includes the painful realities of a broken world.

BROKEN

For 25 years Mary Ellen was married to Frank, a man she calls "the most closed person I have ever met." His tough exterior and solitary personality dovetailed with his military career. But it didn't promote intimacy. Eventually the marriage became too difficult for a very open, nurturing woman like Mary Ellen. "We lived in silence with one another for years," she remembers. "And after a while, silence does horrible things to you."

And so, after two-and-a-half quiet decades, Mary Ellen did the most difficult thing she has ever done: she filed for divorce. Since the kids had grown, she saw no reason to continue the façade.

The separation proved amicable and the two became good friends. He served as her handyman when something broke around the house, and she reminded him to eat right—almost as if they had been lifelong friends who had never married. They lived apart for decades until, in 1999, doctors discovered Frank had a terminal brain tumor. And so, consistent with her compassionate, maternal nature, Mary Ellen took Frank into her home and nursed him through the seven-month ordeal of surgery, radiation, and chemotherapy. No wonder Sharon, Mary Ellen's daughter, calls her mother, "Saint Mary Ellen of Cumberline Gap."

"I'm no saint," responds an embarrassed Mary Ellen. Perhaps not. But she certainly has more of the stuff saints are made of than most of us.

Mary Ellen brought the kids to the Methodist church until her divorce, at which point she gave up trying to practice the faith she had known since childhood. For a while, she sampled a variety of churches, everything from Catholic mass to energetic African American churches—a big step for someone raised in the culture of segregation. She learned to love the tranquility of liturgy and the inspiration of Black gospel music. But nothing ever felt quite comfortable.

I thought of the many boring sermons I had endured while sitting on hard, wooden pews and wondered whether anyone feels entirely comfortable in church. But something deeper than sore bottoms caused by long-winded preachers bothered Mary Ellen.

"Why?" I ask. "Was there a specific reason, or did you just lose interest?"

"I guess I just felt out of place, maybe because church seems more suited to families—there is a stigma associated with being a divorced, single woman." Whether that stigma is real or perceived, Mary Ellen can't say. "I do miss church. I still see myself as Christian. But I worship differently, finding a walk in nature more spiritual than attending church," she says.

Mary Ellen, like several I've met during interviews, feels out of place in church. Like me, she grew up regularly attending. Like me, she once quoted Bible verses and sang Jesus choruses on a weekly basis. Like me, she felt it important to bring her young children to church.

Unlike me, something caused her to abandon the whole thing.

REASONABLE EXPECTATIONS

Did Mary Ellen expect too much from the church? I don't think so.

I ask Mary Ellen to summarize her understanding of essential Christian beliefs. Rather than recite a creed, she offers an expectation. "Christianity is about treating other people with respect and dignity. I wouldn't explain it as beliefs such as the Trinity, but how we live our lives and treat others. But I've seen man's inhumanity to man, including among those who call themselves Christians."

What troubles Mary Ellen most about Christianity?

"I am a very nonjudgmental person. It bothers me when Christians see everything so black and white without considering individual situations."

She cites several examples of people who have experienced some type of rejection, including a friend who was asked not to attend a church-sponsored Bible study after her brother died of AIDS.

"I resent that gays are not welcome within a lot of churches. It reminds me of the anger I felt as a child in the south when my black friend was not allowed to go certain places with me."

On one level, I must agree with Mary Ellen. The church should play a redemptive role in our world, helping to heal the broken, rescue the perishing, love the outcast. I would call her expectations reasonable. And I relate to her outrage when Christians behave in an unloving manner. The largest Baptist church in my segregated suburban Detroit neighborhood refused to baptize African Americans because it didn't allow black members. An effeminate boy in my junior high school got teased and labeled "fag" by other church-going kids. Both make me angry because they run counter to the love of Christ we proclaim.

But I have learned to accept the unfortunate reality that hateful people reside in every group, including churches. I recognize that some people quote the Bible while violating its teachings. I wonder why Mary Ellen hasn't taken a similarly pragmatic view. I quickly discover that her disillusionment runs much deeper.

A NICE GOD

"I can't believe in a God who is a punishing God," she declares. It bothers Mary Ellen that Christians call homosexuality sin. "This isn't a lifestyle that someone would choose. I have several good friends who are lesbian." Her voice becomes hushed at this point to a near whisper. "And almost all of them have experienced some type of sexual abuse."

Once again, Mary Ellen's compassionate heart and concern for hurting people surfaces. She has spent a lifetime accepting those most try to avoid; she has sacrificed herself in order to care for folks most consider damaged goods. Why, she wonders, doesn't the church do the same? She had enough Bible teaching to know that Jesus said Christians should be identified by the love they show for one another. From Mary Ellen's perspective, we must be a disappointment.

I suppose that, given the opportunity, most of us would try to make God in our own image. A God in the image of Mary

Ellen would be a very nice God—one who loves everyone, forgives everything, judges nothing.

I read Mary Ellen a passage from the popular book *Conversations with God* and ask for her reaction to the author's view of the Almighty.

> Evil is that which you call evil. Yet even that I love…I do not love hot more than cold, high more than low, left more than right. It is all relative. It is all part of what is…I do not love "good" more than I love "bad." Hitler went to heaven. When you understand this, you will understand God.[2]

A long silence hangs in the air as Mary Ellen ponders the idea of Hitler going to Heaven. She doesn't want to believe in a God who punishes. But a man who devised the Holocaust should pay. How does one reconcile the desire that God loves all with the need for Him to judge some?

"I don't have an answer to that," comes her honest reply.

"Do you believe in a good God?" I ask, hoping to discover the root of Mary Ellen's hesitancy.

"Yes, I do believe God is good." An effortless reply.

"Do you believe He punishes evil?"

Again, a long silence. I can see in her eyes the wrestling match taking place within. Like the rest of us, she feels intense anger over a man sexually abusing the innocent child or the ruthless leader exterminating Jews and other sacred lives. She wants them punished. But by whom? The God she worships while walking in nature loves and accepts; He does not judge and condemn. My Christian theology says He is both. But Mary Ellen left that view of our heavenly Father behind in favor of one reluctant to scold while eager to console.

"I don't have an answer for that, either." A hung jury.

DISILLUSIONED

So where does all of this leave Mary Ellen, the once-faithful Methodist who now feels out of place among traditional Christians? Would she describe herself as a Christian who has stopped going to church or as a person who has moved away from particularly Christian beliefs?

"My beliefs are not so structured that I'm open only to Christianity," she replies. Clearly, she would wince at Jesus' claim to be the only way. "I wonder why the church is necessary for spirituality. I am not interested in dogma, even though I miss the context and even the ritual of formal religion."

I grew up in a church culture that condemned playing cards, dancing, going to movies, even reading from modern Bible translations. It wasn't easy untangling the culturally-influenced standards of a particular religious environment from larger questions of morality. But eventually I learned to see a world of difference between minor cultural taboos and clear biblical mandates, such as avoiding adultery and homosexuality. And while I feel for those who find themselves wrestling with desires condemned by the Church—I am well aware of the unbearable self-loathing such a conflict ignites—I accept what the Bible teaches.

Many, like Mary Ellen, react against the whole system by lumping the big and small prohibitions together and seeking solace in a God too nice to worry about human failings or sinful choices. The problem, of course, is that such a reaction creates a different, bigger problem. It causes one to feel out of place with a religion based upon the objective, sometimes hard realities of right and wrong, good and evil, love and justice. And it forces people like Mary Ellen into the lingering quagmire of disillusionment.

I wish Mary Ellen still embraced Christianity. She is the kind of person who could be part of the solution for the Church, rather than part of the problem. Her loving heart and willing self-sacrifice would help us reflect a much better image of Christ-like compassion. In fact, I think she retains the residual fabric of Christian belief. That is why Mary Ellen wishes the Church were more loving and becomes angry when some Christians display a critical spirit and fail to fulfill a redemptive role in the lives of others.

Mary Ellen began her story recalling an unpleasant moment when a minister singled her out for failing to raise her hand along with the other kids. I suspect she never entirely outgrew her childhood experience, sitting in church among strict, judgmental Christians. Today, like then, she considers herself a good person, unable to recall any particular sins committed amid her lifelong efforts to love the unlovable, help the needy, and comfort the hurting.

In fact, some even call her a saint.

CHAPTER 6

DABBLERS

AN ASSORTMENT OF APPETIZERS AND desserts crowd the kitchen table, small paper plates balancing on the edge next to a bowl of tortilla style chips and some specially prepared Mexican bean dip. Wishing I had skipped dinner, I dutifully fill my plate and enter the adjoining living room with the others. The setting looks and feels like a typical small group Bible study: a handful of friendly people enjoying high-fat foods and soda while seated in a circle on a long couch and folding chairs. As the only outsider, I can tell the seven regulars feel quite chummy with one another, thanks to years of participation in what organizers label a "Food for Thought" gathering.

I will be interviewing the group, a collection of independent thinkers from various cultural, political, and religious backgrounds who meet monthly to discuss the latest controversy. Earlier topics have included homosexual rights, the place of religion in the public square, and differing opinions on life after death. The city launched these "Food for Thought" clusters in an effort to foster respect and unity in an otherwise divided town. They figured if those who disagree met to chat over soda and Mexican bean dip every now and then, civility might prevail whenever the city council faced its next polarizing debate. Whether the strategy worked doesn't seem to matter to the seven folks gathered on this evening. They just enjoy one another's diverse company.

And I do mean diverse, something that becomes apparent after asking each person to briefly describe his or her current religious status: two evangelical Christians, one recovering Catholic, and four who could be called "dabblers."

I got the label from Neil when he described his own religious history: "I'm not an atheist. I was raised Catholic. I don't go to church or practice any particular religion. I don't know how to define myself. I dabble, I guess." In his late 30s, stocky built with a mild demeanor, Neil looks a bit like the kid in high school who kept to himself. Despite regular participation in mass and catechism during childhood, Christianity didn't take. "When I turned 14, my parents gave me a choice, so I left the church. I didn't buy into it, feeling it was just a story. I'm sure there was a bit of kid rebellion mixed in, but the whole thing seemed weird to me—so I rejected it all."

I ask Neil to describe his "dabbling" in more detail. "I visit the Congregational church downtown once in a while, whenever I hit a rough spot in my life." He explained further, "I've tried a variety of churches, but for some reason I am turned off by those that seem casual and unorganized." He recalls a few incidents visiting Charismatic services. "Maybe it is a carryover from my catholic upbringing, but I think to myself, *This isn't a church. This is a 7-Eleven with a clown. They're nuts!*" I guess Neil feels more comfortable with the sane church he rejected.

Could Neil summarize the basic beliefs of Christianity? He takes a stab. "I think it is just belief in Jesus Christ and His teachings. I don't know all of what goes into that, but He is at the center."

Next to Neil sits Donna, who describes herself as "An unaffiliated, sort-of Christian. Whatever that means." Her tense laughter suggests embarrassment, perhaps worried such a vague description seems unrefined. I get the impression that Donna, a 50-something wife and mother, enjoys hanging around sophisticated people who prop up her hesitant confidence—and that she works very hard to avoid appearing insecure. "I believe in God, Jesus, and the Bible as a source of truth, but not the final source. When I do attend church, which isn't often, I go to the Unitarian Church. A fringe Christian might be a good description."

I suppose you could call Donna a second generation "fringe believer" since her father, raised Catholic, married her German Lutheran mother. Rather than choose between the two denominations, they "did a little bit of nothing" with the kids, making hers a non-religious upbringing. Donna married a man who grew up in and was turned off by the Baptist church, so they followed in her parent's footsteps and did nothing religious with their children beyond Christmas and Easter church visits. "We did teach them the golden rule and the existence of a higher being," she quickly and defensively adds.

"I believe I have a great deal of spirituality," she continues, still defensively. "But to me it does not require church on an every Sunday basis to have a good relationship with God."

"You're a lapsed dabbler?" someone asks with a laugh. The rest of the group chuckles at the label. And since she figures they are laughing with her rather than at her, Donna joins in with a big smile.

As with Neil, I ask Donna for a summary of the basics of Christian belief. "As I understand it," she strains, "Jesus Christ is the Son of God, sent to earth to teach us how to live and how to die. He died and was resurrected so that we could all have life everlasting."

Pretty good for a lapsed dabbler.

Moving around the room, we come next to Wade, a 50ish guy with black hair and dark complexion suggesting an unidentifiably mixed racial heritage, possibly including Native American. I have a hard time following Wade, in part because he mumbles softly, forcing me to strain and repeat my requests in order to catch what he says, but also because he seems intent on avoiding any sort of label or pre-defined box for his religious orientation. He doesn't like me asking about his current religious status.

"Are you talking religious or spiritual?" I've always disliked it when people force that distinction, such as when believers say things such as "I am talking about relationship, not religion." I understand and agree with their point. But the separation feels unnecessarily forced.

"Both or either," I respond, avoiding his trap.

"I believe I am progressing, and I've always been a spiritually sensitive person," Wade begins. I wonder whether by "spiritually sensitive" he means a sensitive heart or something more like a sensitive tooth; does his story hide deep pain? "I am a searcher and a seeker of the truth. I receive spirituality in many ways. I believe that all religions have a piece of the truth and that all deviate a little bit."

Moving from the present to childhood, I learn that Wade has indeed experienced the sensitive tooth of religious abuse. His family was deeply entrenched in the Worldwide Church of God, a highly control-oriented cult led by Herbert W. Armstrong, the man I vaguely recall repeatedly setting and missing the date of Jesus' return during the 1970s. I've met others from that movement, and I see the same look in Wade's eyes—like a cowering, abused puppy who would get defiant if he weren't so afraid of the next slap.

"It is a difficult thing to leave a cult," Wade continues. "Most people have no idea…" His voice trails off, as if the unpleasant memories make it impossible for him to continue this line of thought. He hits fast forward, moving to the next significant scene in his spiritual journey. "During my late teens, after leaving the Worldwide Church, I got into meditation—and I am still searching and seeking. Because of those early experiences, I am not open to the structure of religion."

As I piece together bits of mumbled phrases, Wade's experience begins to take shape. After leaving his parents' cult, he spent three decades avoiding formal religion. (When you have been burned in the bonfire of religious abuse, I suppose even a candle can make you nervous.) He gravitated toward mystical, quasi-pantheistic spirituality, mixed with skepticism. Wade took pride in his tendency to question the motives of anyone considered to be a religious leader. "What I love is what we are doing now," he smiles, "sitting around, informally discussing spiritual matters. I love the genuine. I love the sincere. It's got to be the real thing."

Asked for his summary of basic Christianity, Wade becomes clearly uncomfortable, reminding me that he dislikes boxes. "The definition of Christianity is complete love," he reluctantly offers. "It is to have the entire God living in you."

I try pinning Wade down to something more precise, but to no avail. He seems content with his inability to clearly explain, somehow taking comfort in ambiguity and the eternal "searching and seeking" it allows.

At last I come to Sarah, our host for the evening. A glance at the wall decorations and bookshelf selections suggests that Sarah favors a sort of Eastern religion, perhaps Hindu or Buddhist. Her physical appearance reinforces the notion: a very slight frame, she looks like a former flower child who now eats nothing but organically grown foods.

"I guess, like Neil, I'd call myself a dabbler," Sarah begins. "I don't really believe in God, but I believe in the idea of God. And I can see why people believe because it would be nice to have, but I don't."

I feel surprised that one who believes only in the idea rather than the reality of God surrounds herself with so many religiously oriented paintings and books. The rest of her story helps fill in the blanks. Raised a very staid and stoic Episcopalian, Sarah retains a level of respect for her parents' beliefs.

"Both of my parents are people who I think of as truly religious, in that what they do and how they treat other people has a religious basis. One of the reasons I have some good feelings about Christianity is I see how generous and kind and thoughtful my parents are."

Sarah loves the church her folks currently attend because, unlike so many others, "it welcomes anyone and everyone."

"If there is such a thing as being a true Christian, I'd say my parents are," she continues. "But I think that other religions embody that same idea of treating others the way you'd like to be treated yourself."

Out of the corner of my eye I catch Donna nodding in recognition of the "golden rule" she taught her kids.

"I've also had some influence from Eastern religions that have been really positive," she explains. After college, Sarah went to Nepal with the Peace Corps, where she lived within and among Hindu and Buddhist cultures. She never formally studied the teachings of either, but found herself impressed by belief systems that felt less rigid and structured, more organic to daily life.

"I enjoyed the experience of living among those for whom these belief systems were simply part of the fabric of their society, and that many were Hindu and Buddhist at the same time without seeing a conflict," she explains. Sarah considers the Dali Lama her hero because he seems to live a peaceful lifestyle, even though she never formally became Buddhist.

She also admires one of my heroes, C.S. Lewis. She has read quite a bit of his writings. Maybe that is part of the reason Sarah retains a residue of goodwill for Christianity. "I'm really conflicted," she says. "In many ways, I have somewhat a positive feeling toward Christianity. I light candles for friends who have died. I love the ritual and ceremony associated with religion. There have been times in my life when I have prayed and hoped that it went somewhere."

Curious about what might have pushed Sarah away from the faith for which she retains so much goodwill, I uncover the usual suspect: a college philosophy class that, in her words, "made me think a lot about belief, existentialism, atheism, Christianity, history, and how they are all interrelated." She had a biased college professor, evidenced by her recap of history as a series of atrocities carried out in the name of religions like Christianity.

"I know it sounds naïve to say so," Sarah admits, "but it is hard for me to understand how people who believe in God could do such things."

How does Sarah define Christianity? A long pause suggesting serious contemplation precedes a reference to something a believing cousin shared with her.

"He said that Christianity is the only religion that has complete forgiveness as one of its main tenets"—a good summary, but one Sarah doesn't buy. "I'm not sure I agree with that, but it is one of the things that people say defines Christianity." Almost as an afterthought, she adds a few more defining tenets. "There is also the Holy Trinity of Father, Son and Holy Ghost, that somehow the three entities are one-in-the-same in sort of an odd way. There is life after death, which is not only in Christianity but is, I think, an important part of it."

"Anything specific about Jesus?" I ask.

"Yes, that He actually died for our sins and then came back to life."

Clearly, some of her church lessons stuck. So, where did such an eclectic history leave Sarah?

"I would personally like to think that the Muslim God, the Hindu God, the Buddhist God, and the Christian God are the same God."

"Is that what you would like to think, or what you do think?" I prod.

"Well, as I said, I don't really believe in God. But I think the God that people create spiritually, if there is one, is the same."

I pose one final question to the group. "How do you explain the fact that others fully embrace Christian belief, while you don't? I have spoken to folks with stories and experiences remarkably similar to those you've shared tonight who believe. Why do you think they accept what you reject?"

"The Lord works in mysterious ways," Donna takes a stab. "God exists in all of us, pursues all of us differently, asks us all to follow Him differently because we all have different paths to pursue. Some people have questioning to do in different ways. We all have our works to do, and God has set up differently how He has us do them. Some choose to be born again Christians to know God. Others choose to know God in other ways." According to Donna, who believes in many ways to God, it is His plan for us to choose divergent paths.

Sarah hesitantly offers a different viewpoint.

"I think in some ways it is easier to believe than not believe," she says. "I would really like to believe because I think it would be comforting." In other words, those who believe, do so for the same reason my daughter sleeps with her teddy bear—it just feels better.

Finally, Neil haltingly offers an explanation that he admits could make him sound like a jerk. "What makes me different from those who believe is that they are able to suspend some of their questions, or suspend reality and just say they believe by faith. But I feel like I just can't stop asking questions, and the answers I get just don't satisfy. I don't think I'm smarter or anything like that. It's just that I feel there are a lot of questions that aren't answered, and maybe someone who believes can just take it on faith."

"What a jerk!" someone jokingly jibes. But I appreciate Neil's honesty. His questions haven't been answered to his satisfaction, making it difficult for him to take the faith leap. Of course, as you might expect from the lead dabbler, he doesn't seem serious about pursuing those answers.

As I finish my list of questions, I glance down and notice that I have taken only one bite of each selection scooped onto my plate. I had spent the evening merely playing with my food to keep up appearances. I consider myself in good company: a group of dabblers spending their lives nibbling around the edges of spirituality without ever really digging in.

This approach to faith says, "There is no big story. There is only whatever fable you can piece together from the seemingly random experiences of life." It is like taking ten novels, each with different characters and plots, and ripping chapter one from the first book, chapter two from the second and so on. Hoping to enjoy a new story by reading the excised chapters in sequence, you instead find nonsense and confusion. Rather than experiencing each religious story as written, we have ripped random scenes from various subplots in hopes of creating our own scripts.

But it hasn't worked. And many are facing the harsh reality that treating truth claims as a great spiritual smorgasbord from which to pick and choose is another way of saying none of them are true in an ultimate sense.

Popular novelist Douglas Coupland coined the term *Generation X* in the title of his first best-seller and gave voice to the angst of an entire generation—those whose youth is stained with scenes of the Kennedy and King assassinations, the Vietnam conflict, Watergate, gas lines, and the Iran hostage crisis. Later, in perhaps his most disturbing novel titled *Life After God* Coupland tells the story of a young man wandering from one empty experience to the next in search of meaning or purpose in his life, a man who yearns to run so that his spirit can feel the brisk breeze of joy, beauty, clarity, and vitality. But instead he drags a heavy ball of unbelief affixed during childhood.

"I was wondering what was the logical end product of this recent business of my feeling less and less," Coupland's character reflects in response to the soul numbing routine of daily existence. "Is feeling nothing the inevitable end result of believing in nothing? And then I got to feeling frightened—thinking that there might not actually be anything to believe in, in particular. I thought it would be such a sick joke to have to remain alive for decades and not believe in or feel anything."[1]

This shoot of unbelief sprouted from a very specific root: parents who raised their son without religion because they had broken with their own pasts. Having escaped the rigors of Christian commitment, they set their children free. But unbelief, according to one immersed in its hardening mud, does not free. It entombs. It cuts one off from the cool refreshment of clear direction, keeping one on the rat's treadmill rather than the runner's path. Perhaps worst of all, it makes the inviting notion of sincere belief something beyond comprehension—an internal conflict Coupland captures in his character's offensively effective description of Christian media.

> And there were Christian radio stations, too, so many many stations, and the voices on them seemed so enthusiastic and committed. They sounded like they sincerely believed in what they were saying, and so for once I decided to pay attention to these stations, trying to figure out what exactly it was they were believing in, trying to understand the notion of Belief...I did not deny that the existence of Jesus was real to these people—it was merely that I was

cut off from their experience in a way that was never connectable.[2]

It is one thing to reject Christianity because you don't understand it. It is another to do so because you can't comprehend the experience of real belief—something made more difficult when parents leave you to decide for yourself among religious options so varied that to claim certainty seems naively arrogant at best, dangerous at worst.

I sympathize with the frustration over what seems an endless line of religious perspectives. But there really are not as many as most people think. The modern trend toward relativism has made us lazy by suggesting there are far too many irreconcilable belief systems out there for anyone to compare and contrast. So we throw up our hands and either embrace the one most convenient or ignore them all. We become seekers who will never find.

CHAPTER 7

FREE AGENT

KEN MET ME FOR COFFEE at the local Barnes & Noble bookstore café. He's a technical analyst in the computer industry who doesn't look the part: brawny build, Bruce Willis hair cut, mustache and goatee. He has a sturdy yet warm presence, reminding me of everyone's uncle.

I learn quickly that his 42 years have brought some deep hurts, including a difficult divorce that ripped three kids from his daily life—it's probably part of the reason he seems guarded, as though a seed of mistrust has been planted in the fallow ground of a broken heart. His calm, almost stoic personality dictates that Ken doesn't talk much despite having lots to say. He is a self-described unbeliever who turns out to be remarkably well-informed about the Christian faith.

When I began examining unbelief, I assumed that those who reject Christianity probably do so because they don't get it. They haven't heard or understood the whole story, I reasoned, so they reject a straw man or caricature rather than the genuine article. Ken shattered that assumption, in part because he demonstrated the ability to reference, quote, or summarize scriptural stories and themes better than most Christians I've met. He claims to have read the entire Bible three or four times. I can tell there are parts he has read even more than that.

When I ask Ken how he would describe the basic message of Christianity and how it differs from other religions, he hits the nail on the head.

"Christianity is a monotheistic religion that believes in one God and that God is the creator of everything. It teaches that there is right and wrong, and the wrong is identified as sin that needs to be atoned for. Because people are sinning constantly, God made a means of atonement in the form of Jesus Christ who is part of the Trinity. By Jesus dying on the cross despite being sinless, He was paying for everyone else's sin. Everything they had or ever will do wrong was paid for by that atoning blood. And those who accept that payment are forgiven by God."

Despite a solid grasp of Christian theology, Ken doesn't buy it.

"The Jews hate the Muslims. The Muslims hate the Jews. Christians hate the Jews and Muslims. Nobody can agree on anything; they all seem to hate each other. But there's one thing that they've got in common, and that's God. No matter how wrong those who represent Him might be on their own, God is still right—He still exists."

Free Agent

Today, Ken describes himself as a seeker, but he is quick to qualify the term. He is sorting through several faiths, doing his own analysis rather than following the path as defined by the Christian or any other religion. He's a spiritual free agent.

"I still read the Bible. I think it's a great book. I've read about many other religions, but none of the Eastern religions really appeal to me, such as Hindu." Ken believes in a God who looks very much like the monotheistic God of Christianity, Judaism, and Islam. "And it is important to clarify that I'm not opposed to Christianity."

Ken wants to grow spiritually. He doesn't want to block God's work in his life. "But I don't want to just jump in and go along with the crowd."

I assume he means the crowd of devout Christians, many of whom appear to put faith over reason. He goes on to a topic that touches my own experience growing up in the evangelical church.

"You hear all these grand stories of personal interactions with God: 'God spoke to me,' or 'I had a vision.' And I've never personally encountered anything on these levels. It made me feel that I was missing something or my faith was inadequate."

I can relate. Despite growing up listening to preachers talk about hearing from God, sensing the Spirit, or experiencing an "intimate relationship" with the Almighty, I doubted—sometimes their stories, sometimes my faith. All I knew was that I did not have that kind of drama in my faith life. No voices from Heaven. No supernatural sensations. No faith healings. No life-altering encounters. I just bought the Gospel as truth, leaving me curious why others seemed to get more direct proof-of-purchase. Ken offers a plausible explanation.

"I just figure there are some people who need that kind of thing so much in order to stay engaged and continue their walk with God," he says. "Some people always have to have a problem to take to God. They aren't happy unless they have a problem. One guy I knew always had a health problem, no matter what. He had a bone spur that needed to be shed or requested prayer and healing for a migraine. It was just constant!"

Ken dislikes those whose spiritual identity becomes wrapped up in what God can fix for them. Of course, God fixing man is central to Christian theology. But some bring the concept too far, giving Ken the impression that Christianity is a crutch for needy people.

He also wonders why so few seem willing to answer tough questions. Ken sincerely wants answers.

"I've always heard that we're not supposed to have a vengeful heart," he says. "If someone does you wrong, you're supposed to turn the other cheek and forgive them, understanding that vengeance is God's work. But then I was reading about Samson and how the last thing he did before bringing down the temple was pray that God would give him strength to bring down his enemies. So, if God doesn't want us to have a vengeful heart, why would he specifically empower Samson to get revenge?"

A good question I've never even asked.

"They would tell me, 'Well, those were God's enemies also, and he was doing God's work.' But I still wanted to know why

God would go against His own instruction."

Resisting the urge to defend God, I ask for other examples. He describes a Baptist preacher obsessed with proving they never drank wine in the Bible, despite clear statements to the contrary, such as when Jesus turned water into wine. The preacher had alcoholism in his family, so his passion made sense. But it reinforced Ken's suspicion that the church teaches what it wants to be true, regardless of whether the evidence supports it.

What seems to bother Ken more than shallow, weak, or non-answers is the sometimes defensive, sometimes condescending expectation that he should unquestioningly accept whatever explanation he gets. I can relate, having grown up in a church where we were expected to do likewise. I learned pretty quickly that doubting denominational dogma is a no-no. So I kept quiet, something Ken sees no reason to do.

So what parts of Christianity does Ken find hard to swallow?

"The punishment for sin through a blood sacrifice seems to me very primitive. I mean, we chuckle about people throwing the virgin into the volcano—but it is essentially the same thing, taking something pure and sacrificing blood to make up for somebody else's problems. To me that seems like a very primitive method of thinking."

So what alternative does Ken offer?

"People constantly say that you have to pay for your sins. To me, a sin is its own punishment. If you drink too much, your liver dissolves. If you commit adultery, you risk losing your marriage and children. When you murder somebody, you have to carry that guilt to your grave. So to me, sin has its own built-in punishment."

What about justice? Another reason Christianity bothers Ken.

"I believe God is a perfect judge. He can say, 'You're guilty of this sin, and this is your punishment.' But if I become a Christian and just say, 'Jesus is my Lord,' He'll get me off, scot-free, no matter what I've done. That takes away God's ability to be a fair and perfect judge. To me that is contradictory, because a certain group of people are excluded from God's perfect judgment."

Ken doesn't want any "Get out of jail free" cards in the game.

Is there a single thing Ken finds most troubling about Christianity? His answer came with no hesitancy.

"Its exclusive nature," he says. "The fact that it says, 'We're all going to Heaven and everybody else is going to hell.' That just seems very wrong. If certain people who recognize that understanding and it empowers them and makes them able to follow God, great! I support them in that. But I don't think that you can put God in a box and say that He's never going to speak to anyone in another voice."

Ken offers the burning bush, Jacob's midnight wrestling match, and Balaam's talking ass as evidence that God can speak to people other ways if He really wants to reach them. "I look around at the universe, and I don't see God playing by a lot of rules. He's very versatile, very creative."

Ken's theology can be summarized as follows: God is a personal being who created all things, cares about all people, and can talk to us directly if He really wants to. He is a perfect judge who will condemn sin, which Ken defines as hurting others or failing to do good when given the opportunity. He will not let certain people off the hook just because they claim the name of Jesus. Ken celebrates those who believe as he does in one God, whether Christian, Muslim, or Jewish. They are all on different roads to the same eternal goal. He does not buy any religion's claim of exclusivity. All do their best in the journey toward one true God.

"I guess the straw that breaks the camel's back for me," Ken admits, "is that I haven't been convinced Jesus is the Son of God."

So who was He?

"Maybe He was a good teacher. I'm sure He was a good person. But I don't buy the argument Christians offer that He had to be either Lord, lunatic, or liar. He may be legend, like Paul Bunyon or Santa Claus. Saint Nicholas was a real person, but over the centuries that reality has grown into a person who rides a sled each Christmas Eve, bringing gifts to every child on the planet. The same could apply to Mohammed, a very wise man who said and did many wise things. But a prophet of God? That status may have been attributed to him later."

Did Jesus die on a cross? Ken says yes.

Did He rise from the dead?

"That seems more legend than history."

What of Jesus' claim to be the only way to Heaven?

"I don't believe that He claimed that. That feels like legend."

Is the Bible authoritative or not?

"A little of both. It is a very good source of wisdom in the context of the common mentality of the time. But over the years, it seems there have been embellishments or additions. Two thousand years is a long time for additions to creep in. I view the Bible has containing many things that are good and beneficial. But there are other portions that cause me to doubt."

What traits does Ken see among Christians that would cause us to believe things he can't? Are we needy or naïve, or is there some other common characteristic Ken has observed that might drive us toward belief?

"I sense a common desire for God to save or rescue them from some kind of hardship or need."

"Like an injured person needing a crutch?" I ask.

"In some ways, yes. But not in the negative way that is often used. If they need somebody to encourage them and help them along as a focal point, that's great. And I pray to God and ask for help. But my question is, 'What is it *I* need to do?' Christians seem to leave it to God to do all the work for them."

Ken paraphrases an essay by Emerson titled "Self-Reliance" to summarize his own perspective. "As soon as the man is at one with God, he will not beg. He will then see prayer in all action. The prayer of the farmer kneeling in his field to weed it, the prayer of the rower kneeling with the stroke of his oar, are true prayers heard throughout nature, though for cheap ends."[1]

The farmer doesn't just stand there, helpless, asking God to do something. The farmer's prayer is his work. That, says Ken, defines how he tries to live his own life.

"I pray to God and ask His guidance. But if I sit still and do nothing, why should I expect anything to happen?"

The implication is clear: a common trait that draws many to Christianity is a form of laziness—expecting God to do all the work. Our prayers, be they "plant my crops" or "fix my problem" or "save my soul," suggest an unwillingness to take personal responsibility for our own lives.

Just as I am wrestling to try to understand what motivates unbelief, Ken has tried to categorize reasons for belief. He gives two.

Category one: the unexamined life.

"The vast majority of those who call themselves believers don't know or care why they believe," Ken explains. "They were raised in the church, it was their social upbringing, and they are just following suit. They don't bother to question anything. Ignorance is bliss."

Category two: sincere believers.

"There is another group of believers who are seeking God. And I think that God has used Christianity to speak to them in a way that they can understand. And I love that! God doesn't care about your specific beliefs. I think He cares that you are sincerely seeking Him. No matter how wrong you are, He appreciates that. Kind of like getting a homemade Father's Day card from your kid. The drawing is not going to be Rembrandt, but you look at his desire to please you. How can you condemn that?"

How indeed!

CHAPTER 8

WANDERING

M**Y INTERVIEW WITH JO ANNE** brought me back in time, awakening pleasant echoes of my own religious upbringing: a Southern gospel quartet performing energetic tunes in tight, bouncing harmony; the rhythmic, almost poetic form of preaching that stirred the soul more than engaged the mind; an altar call at the end of each sermon when the preacher appealed to those needing salvation or rededication to "walk the aisle" while the congregation sang each verse of *Just As I Am*. Like Jo Anne, I miss parts of the distinctively Baptist subculture that defined my youth.

Decades later, you might never guess by looking at her that Jo Anne once stood on street corners, handing out Gospel tracts, or entered prisons to help lead inmate church services—part of her training during three semesters at a strict Bible college. You might not guess she taught a Sunday school class when her kids were young. With a charming blend of 60-something sophistication and New Age hip, Jo Anne does not fit the part.

She admits feeling nervous about our meeting because the question I pose, "Why is Christianity so hard to swallow?" represents a lifetime struggle. Jo Anne envies the experience of those who embrace Christianity as a natural, normal part of life. Her story draws me into the stereotypical world of hell-fire and brimstone preaching and guilt-inducing legalism. Several snapshots tell the tale of Jo Anne's journey.

At 13, Jo Anne felt lifestyle whiplash after her older brother "surrendered to preach." The family had been nominal church-goers, able to take most sermons with a grain of salt. Not any more. Big brother became the family thought and behavior police: no more dancing, playing cards, going to picture shows, or "mixed bathing" (allowing boys and girls to swim in the same pool together). So, in the name of holy living, fun was outlawed. Mother could not have been more proud and supportive of her son's newfound zeal, and eventually he went on to become a "big-time preacher" with a large ministry.

At about 15 years of age, Jo Anne participated in a youth group mission to Hispanic and Black families on the other side of her very segregated town: "We were delivering donated coats to their homes, and I was deeply saddened by the devastating poverty I saw. One week later, a member of the church deacon board announced the exciting news that the church had paid off the $60,000 stained glass enhancement project. It just felt wrong."

Wandering

Later that summer, an evangelist came to town for the annual tent revival—always a big event that included Vacation Bible School for the children. Jo Anne volunteered to help the little kids with crafts, giving her an opportunity to observe the evangelist in another context. For some reason, he gave her the creeps. One afternoon when the evangelist offered to drive Jo Anne home, she declined, wary of getting into the car alone with him.

After a short stint in Bible college—the same school her "high flying" preacher brother attended—Jo Anne married a man she met in church. He entered the Air Force, largely at her urging, in order to escape West Texas. While stationed in England, Jo Anne discovered the liturgical environment of the Church of England. It made her uncomfortable, so she took a vacation from church involvement until returning Stateside. There she took their four kids to a mainline protestant congregation where she ended up teaching Sunday school.

Jo Anne can't really pinpoint when she started drifting away from church life. Perhaps it happened during their second post in England or when her husband went to Vietnam or when he returned a heavy drinker. Maybe it was all of the above. Whatever the reasons, her family gradually disengaged, to the point that church became the place for holidays, weddings, or funerals.

I find it telling what people do and don't remember. Jo Anne clearly recalls specific snapshots of the worst moments of her church experience. She has no trouble detailing this or that offense—many of them tied to her brother, the overbearing, successful preacher. But she can't recall an intentional decision to leave an active life of faith. The drift from belief feels ambiguous, with only a few loose recollections to chronicle the voyage.

Today, Jo Anne wanders in and out of an occasional church service, "even the Catholic chapel around the corner from my house," she added with some self-congratulation, pleased by the broad mindedness achieved. "I pray and read the Bible several times per week. I prefer the New Testament. I don't read the Old Testament much, other than Psalm 23. I've always been a searcher."

How would Jo Anne describe her current religious status?

"I would definitely say that I'm Christian, but not in the traditional sense."

Why untraditional?

"I don't like church. But I also feel guilty for not attending, especially on Sunday mornings."

Then why don't you go?

"I don't like preachers who yell. I don't like big churches. I don't like people raising their hands because it reminds me of those holy rollers from my youth. I don't like liturgical services because they feel too cold and stiff." In other words, she didn't like any of the churches she has tried.

Still, it bothers Jo Anne that her grandchildren don't attend church, since "every well-rounded person should be familiar with the Bible." She clearly sees a value in church. I prod further, hoping to discover what has caused such a conflicted response.

"Why do you let service style issues get in your way?"

"I wonder sometimes," she replies. "Especially since I consider myself an open-minded person."

After a reflective pause, Jo Anne attempts to put into words what she feels. "I can't go along with the guilt peddling," she begins. "And I find it offensive that, in my experience, most Christians are very critical and judgmental of others."

When I ask for examples, her preacher brother becomes Exhibit A. "Neither he nor his wife have a good word to say about anyone. And he lives in a gated community!"

Clearly, intense emotion bubbles below the surface, a disgust and disdain that must feed Jo Anne's negative impression of confident Christianity.

"I guess I have problems with Christians who are so sure. Aren't we all seeking? I know I have been."

"What do you think is behind that confidence?" I ask.

"I think in most cases it is because they blindly accept it without really thinking it through. I want to go at this intellectually, making sure it is thought through and struggled through."

Struggled is the key word for Jo Anne. If someone seems unsure, she will listen. If they boldly proclaim with confidence, she won't. It troubles her when believers confidently proclaim Christianity as the only way, something I gather big brother does while pounding his pulpit.

Diving into my list of questions, I discover just how "nontraditional" Jo Anne's Christianity turned out.

"How do you define Christianity?"

"The essence of Christian belief is love. I believe love can conquer everything." While certain the Beatles would concur, I had hoped for something more substantial.

"Forgiveness is a big part of it. God sent His Son to earth to die for our sins, making the ultimate sacrifice," Jo Anne adds, assuring me she retains a whisper of orthodoxy.

"How would you describe God?" I continue.

"God is more like a presence within me, a Spirit. And I believe that He could come in different forms to us." Her answer suggests some influence from Eastern religions.

What does Jo Anne find most troubling about traditional Christian belief?

"The idea that Hindus, Jews, and those who embrace other religions won't have life after death because they believe differently." Her concern for others seems genuine. "That is where I get stuck."

How does Jo Anne reconcile Jesus' statements claiming to be the only way with this concern?

"I can't reconcile the two," Jo Anne reluctantly confesses. "And I struggle with people who accept it so blindly. I guess I have a hard time condemning anyone to hell."

Who doesn't? But some still believe Jesus' claim. Does she?

"I'm not sure He said it," she says, an uncertainty she hopes to preserve.

"Bottom line, why do you struggle with Christianity?" In my final question, I want to uncover the root of Jo Anne's discomfort with the faith.

"I guess I'm too tenderhearted," she replies. "My struggle is that—to totally believe all that Christianity teaches—it scares me. Possibly because I've had so many bad experiences with Christians. I don't want to be like that."

As we conclude our time, I wonder how differently Jo Anne's "search" might have turned out if big brother had sold cars rather than become a "big-time preacher." Clearly, he is a major source of her indignation. One thing seems certain: Jo Anne never wants to find what he has, lest she become what he is.

PART III

ONE WAY

CHAPTER 9

UNSPOKEN CREED

W E ALL KNOW PEOPLE WHO, like those I interviewed, share Oprah's sentiments about God. They want a God who is nicer, less judgmental, and more accepting than the one associated with traditional Christianity. They want Him to value sincerity over accuracy and generic spirituality over dogmatic religiosity.

I believe these attitudes grow out of a desire to follow Jesus' second command to *"love your neighbor as yourself"* (Mark 12:31). Anyone who has watched Oprah in action knows she tries to live this principle. Who can fault her for affirming every person's quest for spiritual growth?

But loving others is the *second* command. We must not forget that Jesus framed it with the *first* command when

He said:

> The first of all the commandments is: "Hear, O Israel, the Lord our God, the Lord is one. Love the Lord your God will all your heart, with all your soul, with all your mind, and with all your strength" (Mark 12:29-30).

Jesus did not command His disciples to love any and every god. Nor did He suggest His disciples were themselves part of God. He commanded them to love God as He is rather than the God we would like Him to be. Jesus pointed His followers to the monotheistic, personal God of Israel, not a pantheistic, impersonal consciousness of which we are all a small part. He did not command us to recognize our essential godhood, but to love the Holy God of Israel.

Jesus also said our spiritual quest includes the heart, soul, body, *and mind*. Spirituality is not a disembodied or irrational activity. It engages all of what it means to be human—including our capacity for reason. He did not invite us to pursue God through a mystical ambiguity, but with an engaged mind—to encounter a real God on a personal level using all of our faculties as human beings made His image. Only then, in the context that affirms rather than sidesteps our humanity, can we properly love our neighbors.

MY STORY

I was born into a family of churchgoers. Like my six siblings, I could recite dozens of Bible stories and Jesus choruses before I could tie my shoes. I look back with gratitude for a mom and dad who cared enough about our spiritual instruction to round us into the station wagon every Sunday, some-times kicking and screaming, to take us to church. If the pan-icked routine my wife and I endure with our four kids bears any resemblance, it wasn't easy. But the process paid off. I be-came a believer. In fact, I became a tiny prophet who boldly proclaimed truth to the pagans around me—creating not a few neighborhood conflicts.

One such incident occurred while walking home from my suburban Detroit grade school, super-hero lunch pail in tote. I passed a group of high-school boys who seemed to be minding their own business, shooting hoops, and drinking soda. But I *knew* they had to be up to no good. Why? Because they looked cool. You know the type: long hair, bell-bottomed jeans, rock music blaring from their eight-track. I had lived in a strict Bap-tist home long enough to recognize evil when I saw it. And so, in a bold move that showed tremendous courage and folly, I cupped my hands around my mouth and yelled at the top of my lungs, "Sinners!"

The puzzled high-school boys looked around to find the source of their condemnation. There I stood, unashamed of my stand for righteousness. They laughed and went back to their wicked schemes, hardly paying me any attention at all. But they made mental note: *the little Bruner kid.*

Over the next several weeks, those boys retaliated against my entire clan. They did nothing violent or cruel, but they did get even. Whenever members of my family walked, rode, or drove by their home, my outburst haunted us. "Sinners!" they would shout. Of course, this required an explanation from me. Mom and Dad corrected my misguided attempt at evangelism. But the neighborhood boys went on chiding until my fed-up father demanded they stop.

That awkward incident sums up much of my experience growing up with faith: confident, in part, due to ignorance. I had no idea what those boys believed. I saw only outward signs that made them different. Maybe they attended a church of another Christian denomination, one that shared the basic tenets of my own. Maybe not. But life in the cocoon of my religious subculture prevented me from looking past obvious differences to any similarities. As I saw it, my church had a corner on the truth—so why bother to examine any others?

BEYOND THE COCOON

As a young adult, I began poking my nose out of the cocoon through meaningful relationships with Christians who wore different labels: Methodist, Presbyterian, Episcopal, Charismatic, and Catholic. I discovered similarities I couldn't (or wouldn't) see before. They may have had long hair rather than short or been a priest instead of a preacher, but they clearly worshiped the same God—often more authentically than I.

My seminary years forced yet another step beyond the safety of spiritual isolation. While my studies concentrated on Christian theology, intellectual honesty required a basic understanding of other world religions. There I discovered, unlike the relatively minor disparity between Christian denominations, fundamental differences. Not mere subplot changes, but another story altogether. Billions of people around the world, over two-thirds of the planet, live their lives according to very different religious beliefs. The inevitable questions came. How could so many sincere people be wrong? Even more troubling, *might I be wrong?*

I realize that asking which faith is right and which is wrong has gone out of style. Skim through the religious section of your local bookstore and you'll encounter an interesting and relatively recent phenomenon. The most popular books on spirituality manage to maintain a polite reverence for all views. Best-selling gurus invite us to glean inspiration from a cacophony of faith traditions, casually hovering over varied religious teachings and texts. Their books make you feel intensely spiritual while maintaining a safe detachment.

I would love to believe that all religions say basically the same thing, that all provide different paths to the same destination. But I can't do so and still take my own faith seriously. If I believe in everything, I believe in nothing at all.

Call me old-fashioned, but I still accept what philosophers call the law of noncontradiction. Put simply, two ideas that contradict one another can't both be true at the same time and in the same way. Despite the mental gymnastics many use in an attempt to reconcile various religious perspectives, distinct faiths offer very different answers to the same questions. One does not respect any by claiming they all say the same thing. Such a view trivializes rather than unites and demonstrates tremendous ignorance of their distinctive beliefs.

My spiritual journey brought me through and beyond such a silly notion to a more mysterious recognition. I have come to believe that all humanity is on a common quest, striving for answers ultimately expressed through the religions we profess. I do not pretend to view all religions as equally valid. But I have come to view their adherents as equally sincere and equally eager for God. We just use different keys to try opening the same lock.

Actually, it was my religious bias that ultimately forced me beyond the safe haven of my religious cocoon. The apostle Paul, the one who told ancient Romans that Jesus is God, shoved me.

In a letter written to his friends in Rome, Paul made a brief but extremely important comment about the human condition. He said that we "push the truth away" from ourselves. Not just truth presented to us, but truth known within us. In his words:

> *For the truth about God is known to them instinctively. God has put this knowledge in their hearts. From the time the world was created, people have seen the earth and sky and all that God made. They can clearly see His invisible qualities—His eternal power and divine nature. So they have no excuse whatsoever for not knowing God* (Romans 1:19-20 NLT).

Notice the expressions he uses. *"God is known to them instinctively." "God has put this knowledge in their hearts." "They can clearly see His invisible qualities."* Paul then explains what we often do with this knowledge:

> *Yes, they knew God, but they wouldn't worship Him as God or even give Him thanks. And they began to think up foolish ideas of what God was like. The result was that their minds became dark and confused* (Romans 1:21 NLT).

Every major religious movement claims some sacred text, usually written by the faith's founder or prophets. Jews read the Torah, Christians the Bible, Muslims the Koran. To varying degrees, the faithful of each consider its scriptures authoritative—God's special revelation—the source of answers to life's ultimate questions.

But in an almost scandalous declaration, Paul hints at a different sort of divine revelation, not written in a book, but on the heart. He claims a universal, intuitive knowledge of God—a truth plainly seen—so obvious it must be willingly embraced or willfully suppressed. Thus, Paul introduces us to the mystery of general revelation—the heart's unspoken creed.

Unfortunately, he doesn't say much. Paul barely touches upon the concept, as if it would insult our intelligence to dwell on the obvious.

Maybe I'm slow. Perhaps I've spent so much time examining the trees of special revelation that I missed the forest of general revelation. Dutifully reading my Bible, I neglected to hear the sermon God has been whispering within me (and shouting around me). A sermon, by the way, He also whispers to the other two-thirds of the globe who do not read my sacred text.

At first, such a notion troubled this recovering neighborhood prophet. But if the Psalmist in Psalm 19:1 rightly says that "the heavens declare the glory of God," doesn't it make sense that the heart would do likewise? And if so, how might we recover its muzzled voice? What beliefs, specifically, do all human beings share? What mysterious truth is written on the tablet of our souls? In short, it can be expressed in three tenets of the heart—simple yet profoundly significant suspicions that encapsulate our quest. The lock we are trying to pick.

Suspicion One: We Were Made for More

Regardless of religious perspective, every one of us senses that life has to be more than meets the eye. We find contentment difficult to achieve because we know we were made for more. The mundane routine of the daily grind doesn't satisfy that deep, persistent longing within. And it never will.

We create wonders that point to the wonder that created us. We tell stories that suggest a transcendent author. We feel emotions that reflect God's tender heart. But most of all, we yearn for something that seems out of reach.

Maybe we are just dreamers, cowards trying to escape the harsh realities of a senseless world. Or maybe a more compelling explanation exists. What if, rather than trying to escape reality, we are trying to connect with it?

J.R.R. Tolkien said it well. "Why should a man be scorned, if, finding himself in prison, he tries to get out and go home?"[1]

C.S. Lewis said it even better. "If I find in myself a desire that no experience in this world can satisfy, the most probable explanation is that I was made for another world."[2]

Deep down, we know we were made for more.

Suspicion Two: Something Is Wrong

After months of joyous anticipation, little Matthew is born. But something is wrong. He enters the world deaf and mostly blind. Years later, he displays signs of what turns out to be a rare nervous disorder. So begins the difficult life of our now 21-year-old nephew.

A relative newlywed and father of 1-year-old Bradley, Don boarded a Phoenix-bound plane a few days before reuniting with his wife and child. He had to get back to the office. Lori and Bradley stayed behind for a second week with family in Detroit. Minutes later, news images flashed across the television screen announcing the crash. A call awoke me that night, informing me that my boyhood pal and best man had died in the flames, along with nearly 200 others.

A small story buried deep within the midweek paper describes how a 4-year-old boy found his father's gun. Lovingly playing with his 18-month-old baby sister, he points the "toy" at her and pulls the trigger. The bullet explodes her laughing face. Police say that when they arrived, the weeping boy cried out to his dazed mommy: "It was an accident! I didn't mean to do it!"

Such moments reveal a world that seems cruel and heartless. One need not celebrate many birthdays to know that we live in a broken world. Philosophers call it the problem of evil. For many, it is the primary obstacle to belief in God. We want good, but see bad. Best-selling book titles reflect our attempts to reconcile the seeming contradiction.

- *When Bad Things Happen to Good People*
- *When God Doesn't Make Sense*

• *Where Is God When It Hurts?*

With so much pain in the world, we wonder, *how can anyone believe in a good God?* Simplistic answers do not work. Philosophical explanations do not satisfy. Compassionate sympathy feels nice but fails to remove the heartache. Life hurts, and we want it to stop!

Sickness. Suffering. Tyranny. Tragedy. Crime. Cruelty. Depression. Death. They all point to the second reality we all know. Something is wrong.

SUSPICION THREE: IT SHOULD BE MADE RIGHT

Like the tension of an unresolved musical chord, the wrong of life creates a yearning for resolution within the human heart. Yes, something is wrong. But leaving it there would drive us mad. We must move on to tenet three. We want it to be made right.

Every "once upon a time" requires a "happily ever after," or we leave the story feeling cheated. Every mother's son killed in battle begs for a nation's gratitude to soothe the pain of loss. Every villain seeking destruction demands a hero seeking justice. Every descent into the darkness of depression pleads in silence for a return to the light of joy.

Even while shaking our fist in anger at a God who seems cruel or distant, we reach for a God we hope can set things right and redeem our pain for a greater good. We don't know how. We don't know when. But we know things should not, cannot, be left wrong. They must be made right again.

The essence of every spiritual journey is a response to these three suspicions. Our faith, or lack of faith, says something to us about why we exist, what is wrong, and how it can be made right again. So does everyday life—answers bubble up in unexpected places. But are we listening?

CHAPTER 10

THE NEW ATHENS

THE COVER STORY DISPLAYED AN odd looking child. At first glance, I thought him a miniature Buddha. Upon closer examination, however, I noticed a yarmulke on his head (that saucer-like cap worn by devout Jewish men) and several emblems around his neck: a cross, the half moon of Islam, as well as a black and white Ying-Yang symbol. Splashed over his image appeared the theme of this particular issue of the *UTNE Reader*, a leading alternative media publication: "Designer God: In a mix-and-match world, why not create your own religion?"

The feature article, "God with a Million Faces," describes what critics call "cafeteria religion" as perhaps the truest spiritual quest of all. Author Jeremiah Creedon writes:

A friend of mine I'll call Anne-Marie is the founder of a new religious faith. Like other belief systems throughout the ages, the sect of Anne-Marie exists to address life's most haunting questions. If I ask her why we're born and what happens when we die, her answers suggest that our time on earth has meaning and purpose. Whether I buy it hardly matters. The sect of Anne-Marie has one member, Anne-Marie, and that's plenty.

But, as the writer explains, Anne-Marie's personal religion did not begin with a voice from the sky revealing God's mind. In fact, there is nothing really original about it at all. That's because it kind of accumulated over time by grabbing bits and pieces from this and that faith.

An artist by trade, Anne-Marie has turned her spirituality into a creative act. Her beliefs are drawn from many sources, some ancient, some new. When Anne-Marie speaks of karma and reincarnation, I hear the influence of Hinduism and Buddhism. Her sense that certain places in nature are sacred is either as new as deep ecology or as old as Shinto. It's hard to say exactly how quantum physics fits into the picture, but she says it does. Beneath it all lies the ethical lexicon of her Christian upbringing, timeworn but still discernible, like the ruins of a Spanish mission.[1]

When asked why she left her girlhood church, Anne-Marie

gets blunt. "I needed beliefs that empower me, and organized religion is disempowering," she says. "It's bogus." Anne-Marie's viewpoint appeared in the alternative press, but it reflects an increasing mainstream trend.

I remember when God made the cover of the very mainstream *Life* magazine. I'm sure it was no big deal to Him, but it caught my eye. In large black letters, the magazine posed a question: "When you think of GOD what do you see?" Inside appears an essay and photo gallery highlighting major and minor faith groups in America, including Jews, Hindus, Muslims, Mormons, Catholics, Protestants, Buddhists, and several less familiar sects.

The essay comes from the pen of Frank McCourt, wildly successful author of the *New York Times* best-selling book, *Angela's Ashes*, a memoir detailing his struggles growing up poor and Catholic in Ireland. This article, like that book, bleeds leftover angst from a man angry with a religious dad who drank his paycheck despite sick and hungry kids—and at a God who would let it happen. McCourt speaks for many who left the church after trying unsuccessfully to reconcile the belief of the faithful with their behavior. In his words:

> So I wrote a book and when I go around the country talking about it people ask me if I'm still Catholic. Well…in a way I am. I drop in to churches. I talk to Saint Francis of Assisi and Teresa of Avila, my favorites. I light candles for people's intentions…But I don't confine myself to the faith of my fathers anymore. All the religions are spread before me, a great spiritual

smorgasbord, and I'll help myself, thank you.[2]

To be honest, something inside me finds his conclusion appealing. After all, there are so many religions out there—who am I to say one is true and the rest false? Even if I wanted to, how does one sort through the haystack of small "t" truths to find the capital "T" needle? It seems much easier and tolerant to pick-and-choose, mix-and-match, live-and-let-live. Maybe Anne-Marie and Frank McCourt are on to something. Who better to decide what's true for me than me? Besides, aren't we all basically saying the same thing?

But something else inside me finds this mindset sophomoric. My spiritual quest has brought me face to face with irreconcilable differences between religious creeds. Only those who choose to remain ignorant can embrace the notion that Jesus, Buddha, Mohammed, and the Dalai Lama sing different verses to the same song. They don't.

So begins the hard work—examining the core message of each. I can do so with an open mind, assuming all may be partly right. But my heart longs for one to ring entirely true, to completely satisfy its unspoken creed.

I consider modern America the new Athens and my spiritual journey similar to Paul's stroll through the Greek Parthenon. The apostle visited Athens as a Roman citizen and a Hellenistic Jew, devout in Judaism, but immersed in the wider culture of his time, including a religious pluralism surpassing our own. The Parthenon provided more than a collection of idols and altars demonstrating the tolerance of a diverse population. It reflected something far more meaningful: the reality and mystery of the one true God.

In *The Decline and Fall of the Roman Empire*, historian Edward Gibbon describes an ancient world of "religious harmony" in which most embraced or at least respected each other's superstitions. The intellectual class participated in various rituals and ceremonies, not because they were devout, but because they were civil. "The philosopher," he explains "who considered the system of polytheism as a composition of human fraud and error, could disguise a smile of contempt under the mask of devotion without apprehending that either the mockery or the compliance would expose him to the resentment of any invisible or, as he conceived them, imaginary powers."[3] In other words, they participated in the festivals and sacrifices because that's what someone from polite society did.

They could do so, of course, because they did not see mythology as religion. Mythology never wanted to be religion, something many forget. Mythology is the work of an artist telling stories, not a prophet declaring truth. I like G.K. Chesterton's explanation…

> He who has most sympathy with myths will most fully realise that they are not and never were a religion, in the sense that Christianity or even Islam is a religion. They satisfy some of the needs satisfied by a religion; and notably the need for doing certain things at certain dates; the need of the twin ideas of festivity and formality. But though they provide a man with a calendar they do not provide him with a creed.
>
> Certainly a pagan does not disbelieve like an atheist, any more than he believes like a

Christian. He feels the presence of powers about which he guesses and invents.

We know the meaning of all the myths…And it is not the voice of a priest or a prophet saying, "These things are." It is the voice of a dreamer and an idealist crying, "Why cannot these things be?"[4]

In short, mythology represents man's attempt to paint a portrait of a God he imagined, but had never met. Only Jews and Christians—both of whom claimed knowledge of the one true God—stood apart. Paganism was not, in their view, harmless superstition. Jews were forbidden to worship a graven image, while Christians considered demons the authors, patrons, and objects of idolatry.[5]

In this context Paul entered Athens, possessing the background and insight necessary to bridge the gap. A Roman citizen, observant Jew, and Christian apostle—his life brought all three perspectives together. The Greeks had one altar to an unknown god. In truth, says Chesterton, all their gods were unknown gods. "And the real break in history did come when St. Paul declared to them whom they had ignorantly worshipped."[6] Paul offered more than just another mythology among many. He claimed certainty, offering a message that "met the mythological search for romance by being a story and the philosophical search for truth by being a true story."[7] Paul created a crisis for the Roman world when he declared that its mysterious god could be known with certainty. That world was never the same again.

The New Athens

Just as the ancient Greeks brought the best of pagan mythologies together into a single, homogenized system, we have created a spiritual melting pot in America. As it should be, religious freedom means we can choose to believe or not believe whatever we wish. But it also places the burden of decision on every individual. And frankly, many of us are too lazy or intimidated to take that responsibility seriously. Like many Athenians of old, we celebrate uncertainty. We applaud those who offer options and invite us to sample all without taking any seriously—thus placing religion in the same category as party hors d'oeuvres. Nice to have, but not essential.

My stroll through the Parthenon of today's religious landscape seems similar to Paul's. Like in Athens, I see many spiritual options. People in my day, like some in his, consider any choice equally valid since none are ultimately true.

But a major and very important difference does exist. Unlike in Paul's era, today's major world religions do not see themselves as the work of artistic imagination. They see themselves as the result of divine revelation. They are not seekers asking questions, but rather prophets declaring answers.

Unlike Anne-Marie and Frank McCourt, I refuse to patronizingly consider all faiths equally valid. That only makes them equally false. We may be saying some of the same things. But that does not make us all the same.

We find humankind's common creed in the questions posed, not the answers given. Yes, we all reach for the same God and try to pick the same lock. But as my journey revealed, clearly we are using different keys.

CHAPTER 11

UNITY?

I F I WEREN'T ALREADY A Christian, I'm not sure what I would make of Christianity. It must confuse observers to try to sort out all of the denominations, doctrines, and differences that have emerged from what is supposed to be a single religion. I am one of us, and yet even I find it perplexing at times.

Open the Yellow Pages of any sizable city in America and you will see what I mean. Under the "Churches" heading we offer more assortments than a Baskin Robbins ice cream shop. If you start your search at the front of the alphabet, your finger will first scan over African Methodist Episcopal. Already you are in trouble, since Methodist and Episcopal show up later as separate denominations. Next comes Anglican, the church our pilgrim forefathers came to America to flee, then Apostolic and

Assemblies of God. Moving on, you will hit Baptist—which subdivides into at least a dozen independent and denominational varieties, including American Baptist, Conservative Baptist, Free Will Baptist, General Baptist, Regular Baptist, and of course, Southern Baptist, the largest Protestant denomination in the country.

Which raises another interesting dilemma: Protestant versus Catholic. You come to Catholic under C. It includes churches with names like Saint Francis of Assisi or Our Lady of Perpetual Help, both of which bother Baptists who consider every believer a saint and who view the Catholic obsession with Mary a form of idolatry. Roman Catholics in turn consider Baptists and other Protestants wayward siblings at best, cults at worst.

Moving on down the list, you will encounter a list of Charismatic churches, which are without question our most colorful variety. You may be familiar with this style of Christianity from watching their more flamboyant representatives on television—the ones with big hair and pretentious sets. But they aren't all like that. Most are very sincere believers who happen to express their emotions more emphatically than the more stoic among us.

From there you can move through the remaining 23 letters of the alphabet to encounter a wide array of other Christian groups—from Greek Orthodox to Lutheran to Nazarene to Reformed—all claiming Jesus Christ as their ultimate head while often accusing the rest of falling somewhere outside orthodoxy. This causes us to spend an awful lot of energy trying to evangelize one another.

Doctrinal disputes fill Christian history. Sometimes the arguments have remained academic and civil. Other times they have not. Today I lovingly poke fun at friends who belong to other denominations. But at times such differences were neither loving nor fun. We even killed one another over whether we claimed loyalty to Rome or Henry VIII, burning "heretics" at the stake.

And yet, Jesus said to His followers, *"By this all men will know that you are My disciples, if you love one another"* (John 13:35). I think we've disappointed Him.

Through most of history, however, Christians have acted like a boisterous family, fighting and arguing with each other over big and small matters alike—kind of an, "I can beat up my kid brother, but you best not try it!" environment. Still, I can't help wondering what those outside our walls must think of all the shouting—or what Jesus must think in light of His prayer, *"...May they be brought to complete unity to let the world know that You sent Me..."* (John 17:23).

I'm glad I became a Christian during childhood. That fact spared me the sifting and sorting process. I simply accepted the version of Christianity my parents offered. We attended an Independent Baptist Church, not to be confused with Southern, Northern, American, Conservative, General, Regular, Free Will, or any of the other roughly 50 Baptist denominations. We considered all of them borderline heretics. Our brand of Christianity featured a very distinct culture. Dad, who served on the deacon board, was called "Brother," as were all of the men. The highest-ranking brother was the preacher, which is what we called him, as opposed to "pastor." And when his preaching was on a roll, he expected and received a congregational "amen" to affirm the point or fill the silence. The music minister led us in hymns like *Onward Christian Soldiers, The Old Rugged Cross,* and of course, *Amazing Grace.* We felt passionate about Jesus. But we maintained our composure and never raised our hands, lest we seem Charismatic.

I got "saved" (the term we used to describe conversion) when I was seven years old by repeating a prayer the preacher suggested. I later walked the aisle—probably during the fifth verse of the hymn *Just As I Am*—indicating my desire and readiness to be baptized. We didn't sprinkle; no good Baptist does. We dunked. And coming up out of the water prompted a chorus of "Amen, brother" from a crowd that considered water immersion the first and most important sign of true commitment to a lifelong walk with Jesus. Not that baptism was the same thing as being saved! We always carefully kept them distinct. I will never forget the preacher's reaction when I walked the aisle and told him I wanted to be baptized. Concerned that a seven-year-old might not fully understand, he asked, "Don't you think you should be saved first?"

"I already am!" came my indignant reply, offended that he would think I had missed a step in the process. Salvation must precede baptism—a point made quite clear even to my immature understanding.

Ours was not a highly educated congregation. Made up mostly of blue-collar workers, we figured if the preacher said it, it must be true. We got strict about small matters like music and hair styles and almost fanatical with non-essential matters like the King James Bible and prophecy.

As an adult, I walked away from that subculture. I saw myself as too sophisticated for its simplicity. But the older I get, the more profound that simple faith becomes. I wasn't taught to respect the depth and complexity of Christian thought and tradition or the rich tapestry of variety the Church offers. I did, however, learn that I was a sinner who needed to be saved—a message, by the way, all Christians embrace in one form or another.

How can a single belief fit so many cultures, styles, quirks, and socioeconomic groups? What at the core of the Christian faith makes it appealing to so many with so little in common? What essential ideas unite such diversity, and how do those ideas differ from other world religions?

The best way to answer such questions is to examine how Christianity responds to the heart's unspoken creed.

First, Christianity tells us we were made in the very image of God. *"So God created man in His own image, in the image of God He created him; male and female He created them"* (Gen. 1:27). Humans were given dominion over everything on earth. We were made for intimacy with the Almighty, walking hand in hand with Him *"in the cool of the day"* (Gen. 3:8), like a beloved child or a cherished bride. I've often wondered what it must have been like to enjoy the sights, sounds, smells, and tastes of a virgin world. What must Eden have been like? It was a place of beauty unlike any we can comprehend, perfectly designed for its inhabitants to enjoy the most satisfying, healthy, adventurous, and pleasure-filled lives possible. It probably had the sandy beaches of a tropical paradise, the breathtaking majesty of the Rocky Mountains, the crashing waves of the Oregon coast, the fresh breeze of an eastern seaport, and the sweet aroma of a Midwestern apple farm.

As originally created, we were innocent beings. Everything in existence was good, a gift from the heart and hand of a good God. Adam, Eve, and their descendants had so much to look forward to! From tasting their first mixed-fruit drink to orbiting earth in a space shuttle, a whole world of discovery, invention, and adventure waited to be enjoyed.

But something went wrong—the second truth of Christian faith. *"For all have sinned and fall short of the glory of God"* (Rom. 3:23). The good God was rejected. Adam, our father and representative, chose to join a rebellion launched by lucifer in which those created removed themselves from God's protective rule. As a result, we live in a world dominated by the opposite of good. Beauty gave way to ugliness, justice to cruelty, joy to sorrow, life to death. According to Christianity, God did not invent evil. Suffering and pain are not devices within the divine torture chamber, used on those who refuse to obey Heaven's edicts. Rather, they're the result of living in a world flawed by rebellion against goodness. And they never were supposed to be part of our lives.

Finally, Christianity answers tenet three of the heart's creed. The "something wrong" must be made right again. *"But God demonstrates His own love for us in this: While we were still sinners, Christ died for us"* (Rom. 5:8). Christianity offers a solution unlike any other religion. Every other faith tells me I must get my act together if I hope to reach God. I must either obey commandments, expand awareness, pay off Karmic debt, or become a better person. But Christianity is not about what I do; it is about what God did. He replaced my despair with hope by becoming the hero of life's drama. He paid the penalty for my sin and rebellion in order to redeem me back to Himself. In Jesus' words:

Unity?

For God so loved the world that He gave His one and only Son, that whoever believes in Him shall not perish but have eternal life. For God did not send His Son into the world to condemn the world, but to save the world through Him (John 3:16-17).

God did not remain in Heaven and bark orders or criticize our inadequate efforts to reach Him. Instead He took the initiative to reach us. According to Christianity, the Author entered the story. God became man so that man could know God.

I've seen the best and worst Christianity has to offer. At times in my life I have grown angry at what I've seen, from silly legalistic rules to serious hypocrisy. Like other Christians, I feel embarrassed by portions of our history—as when the Church silenced Galileo and killed Muslims. I recognize such incidents as anomalies. The history of every faith has moments it would rather forget, when those who proclaim its creed ignore its message. I also realize such failures reflect a truth my faith proclaims: We are an imperfect, fallen race. Still, they make me angry.

Despite feeling embarrassed by some Christians, I've always remained amazed by Christ. And at the core, Christianity is about Christ. Who He is. What He's done. How His life, death, and resurrection answer the unspoken yearning of my heart—and resolve the dissonant chord of my life.

Every religion reminds me that I am made for more. Every religion reaches for God. Every religion offers to make the wrong right again. But only one religion, Christianity, is honest enough to tell me that I can't solve my own problem. I can't obey enough rules, offer enough sacrifices, or become enlightened enough to rise above the wretchedness around and within me. All I can do is humbly accept the redemption offered by the One who made me for more and who heroically sacrificed Himself on my behalf. It's like the preacher told me when I was seven. I am a sinner who needs to be saved.

CHAPTER 12

FROM ONE TO MANY

YOU'VE PROBABLY MET PEOPLE WHO point to disunity among Christians as a major reason they reject the Christian faith. "How can a religion that claims there is only one way to Heaven end up with so many different denominations?" We must address this question if we hope to bridge the chasm between the "many paths" and the "one way" perspectives.

To understand how Christianity ended up so divided, we must briefly summarize our common roots and beliefs. Contrary to popular opinion, all Christian denominations affirm an essential set of beliefs that have been articulated and defended since the days of the apostles.

The modern American political system includes groups with very different opinions on a wide range of issues. But they all participate in a constitutional system established by the founding fathers. The same is true of modern Christianity. While Eastern Orthodox, Roman Catholic, and the many Protestant denominations hold different views on many topics, they all derive their essential beliefs from four foundational touchstones: Christ, Canon, Creeds, and Councils. Few modern Christians realize that these four pillars unified the Church for about a thousand years and remain the foundation for every major Christian denomination to this day. Let's briefly touch upon each.

Christ: The incarnation of Jesus Christ is *the* central event in history. When *"the Word became flesh and dwelt among us"* (John 1:14 NKJV), God revealed Himself to humanity and accomplished His redemptive work on our behalf. All Christian teachings and practices are rooted in the reality of Christ's birth, life, death, and resurrection.

Canon: During the first few decades of Church history, the apostles (those given authority to lead by Jesus Himself) and other first century disciples penned a record of Jesus' life, teachings, and work. They also wrote letters to early Christians clarifying the essential doctrines and practices for all believers. This collection of writings became known as "the canon of Scripture," which we subsequently labeled "the Bible." *Canon* simply means "rule," which says these writings were officially recognized by the early Church fathers as the inspired, authoritative testimony to Christ.

Creed: From the earliest days of the Church, believers recited something called "the Apostles' Creed" whenever they gathered. *Creed* simply means "I believe" and summarizes the common beliefs of all Christians. Remember, it took hundreds of years for the New Testament Scriptures to reach most regions.

They could not refer to a Bible, so they relied heavily upon creedal statements to summarize essential Christian teachings. Even after Scriptures became widely available, this creed continued as "cliff notes" on the key doctrines of the faith. Over time the language of this basic creed became more precise—and the version formalized by the early Church fathers in a placed called Nicea continues to serve as an authoritative touchstone for every Christian denomination. A shorter, earlier version appears below.

THE APOSTLES' CREED

> I believe in God, the Father almighty, creator of heaven and earth.
>
> I believe in Jesus Christ, His only Son, our Lord, who was conceived by the Holy Spirit, born of the virgin Mary, suffered under Pontius Pilate, was crucified, died, and was buried; He descended to the dead.
>
> On the third day He rose again; He ascended into Heaven, He is seated at the right hand of the Father, and He will come to judge the living and the dead.
>
> I believe in the Holy Spirit, the holy catholic Church, the communion of the saints, the forgiveness of sins, the resurrection of the body, and the life everlasting.
>
> Amen.

I should note that the word *catholic* refers to all Christians who submit themselves to these truths. Modern readers might mistakenly assume the phrase refers only to Roman Catholicism. Remember, there was only one, universal Christian Church at the time—so the idea of different denominations would not have entered the minds of early believers.

Councils: During the first eight centuries of the Church, those who had received authority from the apostles gathered as necessary to defend Christianity from the deception of false teachings. "Bishops" from every region met together to form an official "church council"—an authoritative body empowered to resolve serious disputes. They did not occur often (only seven such councils were necessary in the first eight centuries of the church) because the vast majority of believers affirmed the same core beliefs. These "ecumenical councils" continued to provide a touchstone for essential Christian beliefs because they addressed many of the same false ideas that surface in our generation.

- *First and Second Councils:* The first two ecumenical councils (A.D. 325 and 381) assembled in response to the heresy claiming Jesus was man, but not fully God. The authoritative body of bishops clarified that Jesus was in fact fully God.

- *Third through Sixth Councils:* The next four councils (A.D. 431, 451, 553, and 680) all took place in response to the claim Jesus was God, but that His humanity was less essential than His divinity. In each instance the bishops clarified that Jesus Christ was one person who is fully God and fully man.

- *Seventh Council:* The last ecumenical council (A.D. 787)

occurred in response to those destroying religious icons that depict Christ, a movement influenced by Muslim teachings against images. The bishops responded by clarifying that God (who is Spirit) became visible flesh when Christ became man. So they defended using images in worship to affirm the doctrine of Christ's incarnation against the growing aggression of Islam.

During the first one thousand years of Church history, ecumenical councils were only needed on a handful of occasions. Each reaffirmed the teachings of prior councils against some emerging heresy and provided further clarification of the essential doctrines orthodox Christians have affirmed since the days of the apostles. So what happened that caused "one Holy, Catholic, and Apostolic Church" to split into so many distinct groups?

FORKS IN A RIVER

One of the most important dates in Christian history was the year A.D. 1054 when something called "the great schism" occurred between what we now call the Roman Catholic Church and the Eastern Orthodox Church. Tensions had been building for some time between the Bishop of Rome and bishops leading the eastern regions of the Church, including cities such as Constantinople, Jerusalem, and Antioch. The key conflict, however, dealt with the question of authority. The Bishop of Rome claimed final say in matters of doctrine and practice. The other bishops disagreed, claiming only the full council had full authority. They felt no single, fallible man should possess the authority when it comes to the rule of faith.

Precedent for this view had been established in the first decade of the Church when the early disciples encountered a serious disagreement over whether Gentiles must be circumcised for salvation. Even the apostles held different opinions. In fact, the apostle Paul and the apostle Peter got into a public argument over the matter. But neither claimed ultimate authority nor set up his own denomination. They instead submitted themselves to the larger body of "bishops" and recognized that the Holy Spirit would clarify the matter through an authoritative council rather than individual opinions. They allowed an apostolic council in Jerusalem led by Jesus' brother James to resolve the question. (You can read a summary of that meeting in the Book of Acts chapter 15.)

So in 1054 the great river of a single, unified Church became two forks now called the Roman Catholic Church and the Eastern Orthodox Church. No ecumenical council has occurred since that time. Both forks of the river continue to submit themselves to decisions made by earlier councils, but diverge on secondary issues and practices.

The Eastern Church has remained a doctrinally unified group. The Roman Catholic Church, however, ran into problems a few centuries later due to the influence of several corrupt Popes and fund-raising tactics that undermined prior teachings on the grace of God. That's when Martin Luther, John Calvin, and others tried to reform the Roman Catholic Church—leading to what we now call the Protestant Reformation. Centuries later Western Christianity finds itself dealing with hundreds of forks rather than two. Despite the differences between these many Protestant groups, however, it is important to note that they all acknowledge the essential beliefs defined before the 1054 schism.

Imagine a large body of water with a strong, single current. The flowing water finds its source upstream, derived from a lake containing the four Cs described earlier: Christ, Canon, Creed, and Councils. The key beliefs all Christians hold in common were defined, summarized, and defended during the Apostolic and Patristic periods long before any splits had taken place. The 1054 schism and the Protestant Reformation created many forks in the river—but each fork carries the "water" of essential Christian doctrines clarified further upstream.

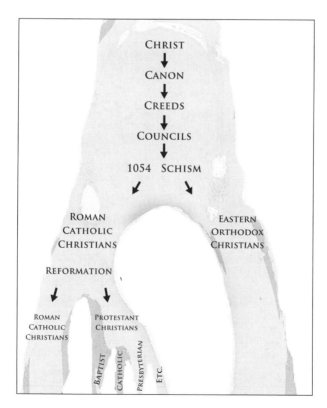

I live in one fork of the river way downstream from the original lake, so I tend to focus on the different shapes and sizes of the splintered forks rather than the common source of water. But we do all share common touchstones for the faith known as traditional Christianity.

In short, despite the many denominational brands of Christianity found in the Yellow Pages, there are not as many conflicting views as might be assumed. And when it comes to the five questions every religion must answer, all Christian traditions can affirm the same basic responses.

CHRISTIANITY IN BRIEF

QUESTION: WHO OR WHAT IS GOD?

Christian Answer: There is one God. He is the perfect Spirit in whom all things have their source, support, and end. He is a personal being, not an impersonal force. He is just and loving and cares about every person.

QUESTION: WHO ARE WE, AND WHAT IS OUR PURPOSE ON THIS EARTH?

Christian Answer: We are spiritual and physical beings created for the purpose of relationship with God. Because we are made in God's image, we have tremendous capacity to reflect His goodness. We have a free will and are accountable to God for our choices.

QUESTION: WHO IS JESUS?

Christian Answer: Jesus Christ is God made man. Born of a virgin, He became human, lived a perfect life, sacrificed His life for our redemption, and defeated death by rising from the dead. The incarnation of Jesus Christ made the way for us to enter communion with God.

QUESTION: WHAT IS WRONG WITH OUR WORLD AND HOW CAN IT BE FIXED?

Christian Answer: Rebellion against God's authority and goodness are the root problem in our world. This rebellion is led by satan—the father of lies. Because our first parents willingly chose to join satan's rebellion, each of us inherits a disease called sin that causes us to tend toward self-destruction and evil. The sacrifice of Jesus Christ frees us from the penalty of sin, and the grace of God frees us from slavery to sin. When we repent of our sin and accept God's gift of salvation, we receive grace to submit to His will rather than our own.

QUESTION: WHAT DOES IT MEAN TO LIVE A GOOD LIFE?

Christian Answer: In Mark 12:29-31 Jesus summarized what it means to live a good life when He said:

> *"And you shall love the Lord your God with all your heart, with all your soul, with all your mind, and with all your strength." This is the first commandment. And the second, like it, is this: 'You shall love your neighbor as yourself.' There is no other commandment greater than these"* (NKJV).

CONCLUSION

CLOSE-MINDED

PRIOR TO MAY 10, 1985, I thought of myself as a fairly open-minded guy. Since then I have become narrow-minded and biased, limiting myself to one possibility out of many. You see, on that day, I got married. And saying, "I do" to one woman meant saying, "I don't" to the rest. That doesn't mean I hate all other women—but it does mean they ceased to be options for me.

The same thing happened when I embraced Christianity as truth. Accepting one meant rejecting others. When we pick and choose from various religious traditions, we do not show our broad-mindedness or inclusivity. We are more like the man who sleeps with multiple women. He doesn't take sexual intimacy seriously. Rather than sacred, he sees sex as a game.

Religion is like marriage. It is by definition exclusive. That doesn't mean a religious person hates all other faiths or even views them as entirely wrong. But we can't view them as equally right. The creed of each excludes the creed of others. Jesus certainly did so when He rejected the notion that all paths lead to God.

> *Enter through the narrow gate. For wide is the gate and broad is the road that leads to destruction, and many enter through it. But small is the gate and narrow the road that leads to life, and only a few find it* (Matthew 7:13-14).

Jesus clearly claimed exclusivity.

> *I am the way and the truth and the life. No one comes to the Father except through Me* (John 14:6).

But Jesus also made His offer available to everyone…

> *For God so loved the world that He gave His one and only Son, that whoever believes in Him shall not perish but have eternal life. For God did not send His Son into the world to condemn the world, but to save the world through Him* (John 3:16-17).

I believe every person is on a spiritual journey, seeking the truth. But for some, the journey seems more like aimless wandering—never reaching the intended destination. Every quest should have a prize. Every search is supposed to find. While I believe all religions reach for the same God, Jesus said they don't all find Him.

On one level, I don't want to hear that. On another level, I know it's true. It *must* be. If we believe in everything, we believe in nothing. Jesus is either who He claimed, or He's an arrogant liar. He died paying for my sins, or He died getting what He deserved. As a Christian, I believe Jesus' claim to be the intended destination of every spiritual quest. He is the prize pursued, the truth sought.

It seems that Oprah and her spiritual mentors embrace Jesus' loving personality, but reject His revealed identity. They quote Jesus' inspiring words, but ignore His clear teachings. As the following summary reveals, their basic creed reflects a very different "religion" than Christianity.

CHRISTIAN CREED	MANY PATHS CREED
We believe in...	*We believe in...*
God, the Father almighty, creator of heaven and earth	An all-encompassing life-energy that has no distinct form or identity. Each of us is a small part of this overarching, collective conscience.
Jesus Christ, his only Son, our Lord, who was conceived by the Holy Spirit, born of the Virgin Mary, suffered under Pontius Pilate, was crucified, died, and was buried; He descended to the dead. On the third day He rose again; He ascended into heaven, He is seated at the right hand of the Father, and He will come to judge the living and the dead.	Jesus is one of the spiritual "messengers" throughout human history, like Buddha and others, who has tried to bring a message of transformation. His followers, however, largely misunderstood and often greatly distorted His message.
The Holy Spirit	A life-force enlivening all that there is.

CHRISTIAN CREED	MANY PATHS CREED
We believe in...	*We believe in...*
The holy catholic Church	A collective consciousness
The communion of the saints	Individual spiritual autonomy
The forgiveness of sins	Higher consciousness through enlightenment
The resurrection of the body and the life everlasting.	Disassociating our identity with ego and physical embodiment.

While I join Oprah in affirming every person's spiritual journey, I agree with Paul when he said the "unknown God" has revealed Himself in the person and work of Jesus Christ.

Is it possible that I believe Christianity to be true because I want it to be true—the wishful thinking of a needy man? Perhaps. But the desire for something does not discredit what you find. Hunger points us to food. Our hearts should want what it most needs. I can't ignore the claims of Jesus and pretend to respect His teachings. None of us can. That's why I resonate with comments made by two men who once rejected the Christian faith, but later became its most articulate spokesmen.

C.S. Lewis said it like this:

> I believe in Christianity like I believe that the sun has risen, not only because I see it, but because by it I see everything else.[1]

G.K. Chesterton said it even better:

> Because it fits the lock; because it is like life. It is

one among many stories; only it happens to be
a true story. It is one among many philosophies;
only it happens to be the truth. We accept it;
and the ground is solid under our feet and the
road is open before us.[2]

The road is open before us. Christians do not need to live a
close-minded life. God may not be in all things, but He can and
does speak through all things. The atheist has to see most of the
world as mad or delusional. The Christian, on the other hand,
is free to hold a more liberal view—to see others as partly right
because they've picked up bits and pieces of truth that resonate
with the heart, pointing them to a God who fits the lock of our
common spiritual yearning.

ENDNOTES

INTRODUCTION

1. Oprah television show clip posted at www.youtube.com/watch?v=317R0keK9x8&feature=related (accessed April 28, 2010).

CHAPTER 1

1. http://www.worldometers.info/books/ (accessed April 28, 2010).aa

2. http://www.bowker.com/index.php/component/content/article/14/131 (accessed April 28, 2010).

3. Oprah.com Spirit Channel at iTunes.

4. Oprah's Soul Series Podcast—Episode 1 (iTunes).

5. Eckhart Tolle, *A New Earth* (New York: The Penguin Group Publishing, 2005), 274-275.

6. http://www.eckharttolle.com/home/about/eckhart tolle (accessed April 28, 2010).

7. Tolle, 6-7.

8. *Ibid.,* 3-4.

9. *Ibid.,* 4.

10. *Ibid.,* 13-16.

11. *Ibid.,* 18.

12. *Ibid.,* 196.

13. *Webster's New World Dictionary* (New York: Warner Books, 1984), 196.

14. Tolle, 6, 27.

15. *Ibid.,* 9, 22.

16. *Ibid.,* 12, 73.

17. *Ibid.,* 15.

18. *Ibid.,* 276.

19. *Ibid.,* 22.

20. *Ibid.,* 74, 276.

21. *Ibid.,* 18.

22. Oprah's Soul Series Podcast—Episode 1 (iTunes)

23. Tolle, 21, 70.

24. *Ibid.,* 23.

25. *Ibid.,* 16.

26. *Ibid.,* 52-57.

27. *Ibid.,* 28, 81.

28. *Ibid.,* 254-259, 271-272.

29. *Ibid.,* 280-281.

30. *Ibid.,* 6.

31. Oprah's Soul Series Podcast, Episode 1

32. Tolle, 309.

Chapter 2

1. http://eomega.org/omega/faculty/viewProfile/aad265 8b4a173589f57dd7f1b83e02a4 (accessed April 28, 2010).
2. Elizabeth Lesser, *The Seeker's Guide* (New York: Villard Books, 1999), 4-5.
3. *Ibid.*, 8-12.
4. *Ibid.*, 15.
5. *Ibid.*, 16-17.
6. *Ibid.*, 18.
7. *Ibid.*, 18.
8. *Ibid.*, 23.
9. *Ibid.*, 25.
10. *Ibid.*, 51.
11. *Ibid.*, 28.
12. *Ibid.*, 70.
13. *Ibid.*, 29.
14. *Ibid.*, 330.
15. *Ibid.*, 330.
16. *Ibid.*, 325.
17. *Ibid.*, 332.
18. *Ibid.*, 61.
19. *Ibid.*, 133-138.
20. *Ibid.*, 213.
21. *Ibid.*, 241-242, 281.
22. *Ibid.*, 328-333.

23. *Ibid.,* 328.

24. *Ibid.,* 341-342.

25. *Ibid.,* 328.

CHAPTER 3

1. Michael Bernard Beckwith, *Spiritual Liberation* (New York: Atria Paperback Books, 2008), 1.

2. *Ibid.,* xvii.

3. *Ibid.,* 3-4.

4. *Ibid.,* 5.

5. *Ibid.,* 7.

6. *Ibid.,* 10.

7. *Ibid.,* 8.

8. *Ibid.,* 1.

9. *Ibid.,* xvi.

10. *Ibid.,* 2.

11. *Ibid.,* 1.

12. *Ibid.,* xvii.

13. *Ibid.,* xviii.

14. *Ibid.,* 7.

15. *Ibid.,* 2.

16. *Ibid.,* 6.

CHAPTER 4

1. http://www.oprah.com/spirit/What-is-the-Meaning -of-Spirituality-Video (accessed April 28, 2010).

2. John Shelby Spong, *Jesus for the Non-Religious* (New York: Harper Collins Publishers, 2007), xiv.

3. *Ibid.,* 8.

4. *Ibid.,* 9.

5. *Ibid.,* 9.

6. *Ibid.,* 214.

7. *Ibid.,* 11.

8. *Ibid.,* 272.

9. *Ibid.,* 275.

10. *Ibid.,* 289-290.

11. John Snelling, *The Buddhist Handbook* (Rochester, NY: Inner Traditions International, 1991), 43-54.

12. *Ibid.,* 3-4.

13. *Ibid.,* 4.

14. *Ibid.,* 7.

CHAPTER 5

1. I have changed names and some details to protect confidentiality, but the stories told and words spoken are 100 percent true.

2. Neale Donald Walsch, *Conversations with God* (New York: G.P. Putman's Sons, 1996), 36.

CHAPTER 6

1. Douglas Coupland, *Life After God* (New York: Pocket Books, 1994), 178.

2. *Ibid.,* 182-183.

Chapter 7

1. *The Portable Emerson* (New York: Penguin, 1957), 157.

Chapter 9

1. J.R.R. Tolkien, *The Tolkien Reader* (New York: Ballantine Books, 1966), 79.

2. C.S. Lewis, *Mere Christianity* (New York: Simon & Schuster, 1996), 121.

Chapter 10

1. Jeremiah Creedon, "God with a Million Faces," *Utne Reader* (August 1998), 42-44.

2. Frank McCourt, "God in America," *Life* (December 1998), 63-64.

3. Edward Gibbon, *The Decline and Fall of the Roman Empire* (New York; Penguin, 1980), xx.

4. G.K. Chesterton, *The Everlasting Man* (San Francisco; Ignatius, 1925), 108.

5. Gibbon, 262-270.

6. Chesterton, 110.

7. *Ibid.*, 248.

Conclusion

1. C.S. Lewis, *The Weight of Glory* (San Francisco: Harper Collins, 2001), 140.

2. Chesterton, *The Everlasting Man* (San Francisco; Ignatius, 1925), 249.

ABOUT THE AUTHOR

I invite you to explore Christianity further by listening to my free podcast. Learn more by visiting my Website:

WWW.KURTBRUNER.COM